BEYOND BRANDING

HOW SAVVY MARKETERS BUILD BRAND EQUITY TO CREATE PRODUCTS AND OPEN NEW MARKETS

Joe Marconi

PROBUS PUBLISHING COMPANY
Chicago, Illinois
Cambridge, England

ISBN 1-55738-428-2

Printed in the United States of America

BB

CTV/BJS

1 2 3 4 5 6 7 8 9 0

*To my children
and to the memory of my parents
who would have liked my books
and loved my children*

Contents

Section II

Going Beyond Branding

Section III

Creating, Managing, and Marketing Brand Equity

Contents

PREFACE

A brand is a name. Brand equity is the value of that name. This book is about creating, managing, and marketing brand equity.

In the 1990s, business has focused its attention on the matter of brand equity, making it a hot subject with long, rambling definitions and descriptions. This book is primarily aimed at marketers. Once pretty much limited to considering pricing and distribution, today's marketing professional seeks to bridge the gap between high-tech and personal service with research, publicity, and advertising. A solid marketing plan will also include graphics, packaging, and positioning. A strategy should govern the marketer in all these areas.

The marketer is also a key player in product development, both initially and in brand extensions.

What does the public want?

Are current products and services meeting needs? If not, what can be done about it?

Is it time for something new and improved? A companion product? A whole new line . . . or just a new wrapper and logo?

What's your "good name" worth to dealers, retailers, consumers and franchisers?

And what about shifting gears entirely—taking your business name into a whole new field?

Brand equity has grown in importance in business locally and worldwide. Billions of dollars are invested in building brands and the suggestion of value that goes with them. Sometimes companies are sold and the original flagship products are quickly abandoned. It was the trusted company *name* the buyer wanted.

But times and tastes change. To stay alive, it's sometimes necessary to diversify. When diversification is the order, is it better to buy or build? It depends on a number of considerations. How would an increasingly health-conscious public feel about the R.J. Reynolds Cookie Company? Better to buy the company and keep the name Nabisco. Moviegoers were thought to respond better to "Columbia Pictures presents ... " over a theater marquee than to "a Coca-Cola Company release."

Even the most astute among the multi-nationals are becoming more familiar with psychographic impressions. Mitsubishi, for instance, wears fine on a plaque of a jet engine or a motor car, but for a beer ... let's call it Kirin. Yamaha, on the other hand, is a highly respected nameplate on pianos and motorcycles. They worked hard at making it so.

We look at names, logos and corporate identity programs, franchising, mergers, name changes and, perhaps most importantly, brand building and extensions of the brand. We will examine vanity and practicality and why the Coca-Cola Company found more success in Diet Coke than it did in Tab. And why Trump Airlines never caused sleepless nights at United.

As a prominent design firm's president noted, "The incredible costs of introducing new brands points out the need to hitchhike on what already exists."

I prefer the term *build on* to hitchhike, to take a brand name and go *Beyond Branding*.

Thanks to Ron Cohn, Dr. Bob Bailey, Dennis Chase, Ron Cox, Tom Lohr, Steve Simon and Katie Spencer (Johnson).

The Best Names in the Business

A very seasoned and respected marketing professional was heard to say "People don't buy brands, they buy products. Keep the focus on the *product*." That's a good line—and certainly quotable—but, like so much else these days, it's a bit too simple.

Certainly, people buy products, but *which* products they buy and how they make their buying decisions has a lot to do with how they feel about the brand. Huge budgets go for advertising, promotions, and publicity each year for some very successful companies. They allocate these budgets to become better known because it is increasingly more accepted that, in the minds of the consumers, a *better-known* brand is thought to be a *better brand*.

Think of the best names in the business—any business. How did they get to be the best names? Imagination, quality and style had a lot to do with it. But much energy was dedicated to defining (1) *what* people will think of the brand and (2) *how* people think of the brand.

How important is brand image?

Very important. It's usually what people remember, if they remember anything at all.

In 1992, the press secretary of the President of the United States sought to distinguish between the two major political parties. He told a reporter "They're the 'New Generation' and we're 'The Real Thing,'" using the high visibility image lines of cola war rivals Pepsi and Coke. On that same day, on NBC television's *Meet the Press*, Texas Governor Ann Richards talked about political campaign tactics, saying "It's like 'Things go better with Coke.' You hear it enough and it permeates you."

Sometimes brands truly do permeate and become so familiar they become synonymous with their product category and can appear generic. Coke, Kleenex, and Xerox are constantly battling to protect their trademarks and make the distinctions that they are not categories, but *brands*.

Adweek magazine underscored the importance of this subject when, on July 13, 1992, it revamped its *Adweek's Marketing Week* spin-off and reintroduced it as *Brandweek*.

It is important to understand the intrinsic value in the brand. Harvard is regarded as one of the world's greatest universities, but when it allows its name to be used on a repackaged multi-volume set of great books (*The Harvard Classics* from Grolier) or on sweatshirts sold in airports and department stores or on a nationally distributed humor magazine, it is using/selling/exploiting the value of its name—its brand name.

Money is a brand of a personal finance magazine.

Advertising Age and *Adweek* are competing brands of trade publications.

CBS is a brand in broadcasting and, while it may argue the point, it exploits it as such to suggest a certain level of quality and integrity, especially in its news and documentary programming. Like Harvard, it wants its audience to accept that a certain high standard of quality can be assumed just on the basis of its name.

And business is only just beginning to realize the potential of an established good name in the form of brand extensions—from cigarettes to fashions.

An *Advertising Age* headline read "Brand Extensions Take Center Stage" and noted how marketers were hard at work to develop superbrands, megabrands, and master-brands—global, multi-product/multi-category lines.

Joe Cappo, publishing director of *Advertising Age* and author of *Future Scope: Success Strategies for the 1990s & Beyond*, says "Companies that fail to respond to changes in the marketplace are in danger of losing market share or even going out of business." He adds "Marketers and merchandisers should develop products and services that fill specific niches and subniches in the market."

The era demands more. Despite the high cost of doing business and the high failure rate, there is a rush of new products each year, and many of them have very familiar names: Oreo, America's best selling cookie for years, is now available in "double-stuffed" (that's with extra cream filling), covered with dark chocolate *or* with white chocolate, over-sized or minisized; Grey Poupon, the premium mustard, ventured into a line of salad dressings; McDonald's, the fast food giant, which already introduced its own line of clothing, licensed its name to Mattel for a new line of toys; Bausch & Lomb, the eyecare products company, entered the mouthwash business; and Arm & Hammer, the company that for years recommended its baking soda be used as a room deodorizer or a toothpaste, brought out a line of toothpaste.

It's too early to judge the success of these ventures, but obviously some will make it and some won't. And for those that don't, there'll be new issues to take their place.

With due respect to the various brands referenced in this work, some are little more than anecdotes because they represent opportunities taken or missed . . . and there's not an awful lot more to say about them. Others are among the greatest success stories or biggest failures—and they have been singled out for considerably more detailed examinations. Some, like Marlboro, Coke, and Pepsi, are more than brands and have become so wildly successful on a global scale as to be virtual "institutions" on a level to which other brands aspire.

In 1988, *Chicago Tribune* marketing columnist George Lazarus closed his book *Marketing Immunity* with the observation that "There's no scientific formula marketers can use to know when they should roll the dice. But marketers who keep their eyes and ears open should gain a sense of when the time is right."

That seems like a good point on which to begin.

Section I

ABOUT BRAND NAMES, PARTS, LOYALTY, AND TROUBLE

Chapter One

THE RIGHT NAME

*"You're not famous until
my mother has heard of you"*

—Jay Leno

Starting With the Right Name:
The Cornerstone of Brand-Building

Once the *idea* of a product or service turns into the actual product or service, the next area of attention becomes choosing the right names. Having the right name is about as important as the product.

Some brand names become so big they become the names of their product categories. We say *Coke* and *Kleenex* and *Xerox* when referring respectively to any cola beverage, facial tissue, or photocopy. But most products have to work hard to be noticed at all, much less stand out from the pack. Some poke fun at themselves trying to make you remember their names. ("With a name like Smuckers it's got to be good.") Some spell it out for you. (How do you spell relief? R-O-L-A-I-D-S.) Many others set their names to music you'll remember. Others name themselves for your town, your state or someone you love and respect: *New York Life, Illinois Toolworks, Mother's Oats,* and *Lincoln Savings* are a few examples.

Charles Schwab, America's most successful discount stockbroker, says two of the smartest moves he's made were naming his firm after himself and using his photograph in his ads. The theory was that people wanted to know the names and faces of people they'd be asking to handle their money. The name, the face, and the focus of the campaign suggested integrity and trustworthiness. It helped, of course, that Schwab's name was simple and easy to say and that he was a pleasant-looking, photogenic man. After Mr. Schwab named his "brand" for himself, he then had to build it to prominence.

A case of "instant brand building" was when actor Paul Newman put his name and face on the jars of Newman's Own salad dressing, sauces, popcorn, salsa, and other products. In his case, it worked.

Helen of Troy hair care appliances saw sales increase some twelvefold over little more than a decade (to $117 million in 1991) after it added the name of Vidal Sassoon to its packaging. The image and reputation of the legendary stylist instantly became the reputation of the hair dryers and curling irons by association.

The new business start-up or young company without an identity in the marketplace should give selection of a company name and a product name the attention it deserves. The following are some key considerations in choosing a name:

➡ Your company name should suggest stability and integrity.

➡ Your product name, when possible, should say something about the product. (Some examples are

Fix-O-Dent denture adhesive, Jiffy Lube auto service, or Golden Grain Rice.)

➡ Avoid negative imagery or identification in the product name. (AYDS weight loss candy and wafers is an example of an especially unfortunate product name.)

➡ Try to avoid acronyms. For every IBM there are hundreds of meaningless, forgettable amalgamations of letters that say nothing about who you are or what you do. Okay, you can buy a PC from IBM, but how many more can you name? People buy products and service from companies with names.

➡ Historically, products have achieved a high level of recognition when named for a person and accompanied by a photo or illustration (such as Betty Crocker, Mama Celeste, Chef Boy-ar-dee, Buster Brown, Uncle Ben's, Peter Pan, Duncan Hines, Dean Witter, PaineWebber, Merrill Lynch, Ralph Lauren, and Colonel Sanders).

➡ Upbeat and cheerful names historically outdo bland names. Health benefits notwithstanding, Cheerios have always outsold 40% Bran Flakes and the Chevrolet Impala always outpaced the same company's Biscayne, even though the designs were similar and the latter lower priced.

This is essentially the basic advice for choosing a name: simple is better than complicated; few letters or words are better than much longer names; light, upbeat names are better than heavy, pompous names; try to tell what the product is or does in the name; when possible, suggest or state a benefit; whenever you can, allude to being big, stable, and worthy of the customer's attention and purchase price.

Some names are chosen to instantly communicate a message and to create an impact—names like Brut and Obsession. Consider the difference in impact between calling a particular perfume Elizabeth Taylor's Perfume or Elizabeth Taylor's Passion.

The Corporate Parent/Child/Sibling

Usually, corporate family relationships are beyond the control of the marketing department, yet they frequently pose challenges, problems, and more than an occasional dilemma.

The New York Palace Hotel had to change its name from the Helmsley Palace because the parent company's name was so mired in bad public relations, it kept people away from a perfectly fine property.

The mere announcement that Rupert Murdock had purchased the *Chicago Sun-Times* caused the well regarded newspaper's circulation to plummet.

For several years, the Nestlé Company was the target of an international boycott because the division of the company selling infant formula in third world countries came under severe criticism. As a result, thousands of people (or more) wouldn't support well-liked, high-quality products and services including candy bars, hotels, restaurants, and a premium line of frozen foods.

Beatrice Companies hoped to raise its book value to investors by emphasizing its ownership of companies from detergent producers to dairies to candy and more. The public, correctly seeing no connected benefit to them in this information, greeted the campaign with resounding indifference.

Our subject is brand building—making a product stand for something thus causing people to buy it and to keep buying it. If identification with a parent company is going to help further that aim, do it. If such identification will be a negative, a mere exercise in ego gratification, or if it could cause the consumer to react with "So?" choose another approach.

For years, General Motors, despite design similarity and no attempt to keep corporate parentage a secret, marketed each of its cars so strictly independent of one another that the only mention of GM was in the fine print copy of the owners' manuals. Owners of a Pontiac, Oldsmobile, Buick, Cadillac, or Chevrolet would, to varying degrees, exhibit fierce loyalty to their brand of choice and disdain for the other makes, priced a few thousand dollars apart—even when it would be revealed several used interchangeable parts. The owner's choice of car was (is) often a statement of taste and status as well as transportation, something not to be confused or trifled with. A brief campaign built around "The GM Mark of Excellence," a rare attempt to wave the corporate flag to attract investors and cross-over service department business, failed when the frequent "recalls" of numerous makes and models suggested the mark of excellence was likely to fall off in the driveway.

Of course, it would be perfectly fine for General Motors to say it had a car for every budget and lifestyle and market its lines accordingly, but the lines are often blurred as the products seemed designed to compete with one another and dealers fiercely undercut sister-company car prices.

Interestingly, Saturn, GM's first new line in three generations, achieved initial great success—outshining other GM makes—with a marketing plan that deliberately distanced itself from the GM name and image.

The reasons to emphasize or exploit parent company, sister-company, and divisional relationships are:

1. To emphasize bigness, suggesting stability and dependability

2. To hype the value of parent-company stock by generating the highest possible level of awareness

3. To leverage the perceived importance of the separate or combined companies to create greater buying power, shelf space, or category dominance.

Identifying companies with one another, however, is a double-edged sword. Bigness raises consumer (as well as retailer and media) expectations. Those trash bags had *better* be of the highest quality if they are manufactured by a division of Mobil Oil Corporation! The marketplace will immediately pay greater attention to a product that's "new from. . ." a major, well-respected company, but they will quite correctly expect in return for that instant attention a higher quality product than from a totally unfamiliar name.

In an earlier book, *Crisis Marketing: When Bad Things Happen to Good Companies*, I showed how Tylenol not only survived, but grew stronger following the deaths of several persons who had ingested tainted capsules. The manufacturer exploited the historic reputation of its parent company, Johnson & Johnson. Most everyone seemed willing, even eager, to exempt from blame a company whose ethics and adherence to the highest quality standards over the years put them above reproach. A lesser company, with a lesser reputation, would have been put out of business by the public's rejection, if not lawsuits. Tylenol used Johnson & Johnson's good name as a safety net and went on ultimately to win over an even larger share of the market.

The Ford Pinto had a serious defect. Upon impact, in addition to the usual dented fenders, the gas tank exploded, bursting into flames. Ford discontinued the model and responded to the lawsuits, but its public relations campaign emphasized its good name and the goodwill the company had built up over the years. Not only did Ford survive but in 1992, the company earned respect and admiration when its Taurus model became the best-selling car in America, an honor foreign automakers had claimed for several years.

Could any company have fared as well?

Maybe. But more likely not. A large company with a history and a reputation—a good name upon which to draw—began its defense miles ahead of an unknown commodity.

Advertising has a "halo effect" where a product or company can benefit from the glow of another company:

⇒ Snickers from the makers of Milky Way

⇒ Roseanne from the producers of The Cosby Show

⇒ IBM typewriters from the leaders in computers

These aren't brand extensions; they're examples of using the successes of one product to launch another wholly dissimilar product, to suggest that the new entry is easily in the same quality class as the established name. It's a very good strategy requiring merely that both the established product and the new product be very good.

Van Kampen Merritt is a very successful company in the investment trust and mutual fund business. When Xerox, America's leading name in copying machines, bought the firm, they added the line "a Xerox Financial Service Company" under the Van Kampen Merritt signature in advertising, on letterheads, and anywhere else the name appeared. For a considerable amount of time, the company debated just how large or how small the Xerox name should be in relation to the lesser-known division. In an independent research study, one comment was offered enough times to make the point clearly: Xerox is a good name that stands for quality, integrity, and stability. Good. But just because they're tops in manufacturing office copy machines ("Xerox machines") how do we know they know anything about running a mutual fund company?

The decision was clear. Use the Xerox name in the ads to suggest a strong and stable parent, but not so prominently that the parent overshadows the division, calling attention to the fact that these two companies have basically nothing in common. While this practice was not followed uniformly among all Xerox Financial Services companies, it was the right course for Van Kampen Merritt.

Often the corporate parent's name will not appear anywhere in the ads, labels, or product literature when the dissimilarity is so great that calling attention to it might seem curious or even embarrassing. An example of this is Coach, the company that manufactures and sells, often through its own fashionable shops, fine leather products. These products are *so* fine as to have a definite snob appeal in handbags and briefcases, to name two major profit areas. Given these circumstances, it may surprise many to learn that Coach's parent company is Sara Lee, the midwestern organization largely known for its cheesecake and other dessert and food products. It should surprise no one that Sara Lee doesn't see any obvious advantage to putting its name on Coach's merchandise.

Quite simply, the overall guiding principle in how the parent companies should publicly define their relationship with their subsidiary companies and the subsidiaries with one another should be based on clear and distinct advantages to both.

Is There a Benefit?

Tylenol was saved from certain disaster by having Johnson & Johnson for a parent.

Coach would likely benefit not at all from its Sara Lee identification.

The infant formula problems—a marketing misstep of grand proportions—caused a worldwide boycott that affected all divisions and products of Nestle.

GM's name on the mailboxes of its five established divisions was a mixed blessing, inviting both passionate loyalty and fierce rejection. Saturn's lack of GM identification doesn't seem to have hurt it.

If the benefit is to one or both components in the relationship, exploit it, advertise it, and cherish it. If the benefit can't be clearly defined, don't let vanity get in the way of your marketing effort.

How It Plays on the Stock Exchange

When is the premise that both the parent company and its subsidiary should both benefit invalid? When the goal is solely to boost the company stock.

A bakery and a leather company might be unlikely partners in the minds of consumers, but if both are profitable and owned by the same entity, this is big and important news to the stock analysts.

Typically, touting corporate performances is the editorial province of *The Wall Street Journal* and national business magazines such as *Business Week, Fortune,* and *Forbes.* When the ever vigilant business press somehow fails to notice a company, and its publicity representative doesn't quite feel he or she got the attention the story deserves, these same publications have been only too willing to accept paid ads reporting which mutual fund was number one according to various rating services and who just posted record profits for the 400th consecutive quarter.

Additionally, companies far from being household names have taken their tale to television screens. Archer-Daniels-Midland, for example, is a major supplier of raw materials to a wide variety of industries, while offering consumers no brand of their own. Why then is ADM a major sponsor with slickly produced TV spots on all networks' major Sunday national news shows? Because these shows are watched in large numbers by people who evaluate and buy stock. They are also watched closely by regulators and members of legislatures, two groups ADM very much wants to please. The other group staring at the screen includes corporate and business types of a caliber ADM just might want to recruit one day or whose company it may want to buy.

For at least a couple of these reasons, Merrill Lynch, Dean Witter, AFLAC, the Chubb Group of Insurance Companies, and General Electric are frequent Sunday morning TV news and public affairs show advertisers. Pepsi, Coke and major snack foods are not. Their efforts are directed at the retail consumer level.

Logos and Signatures and Acronyms

Some ad historians believe the very concept of the brand began with the creation and use of the logo. That symbol, that identifying mark, distinguished one product from another. Indeed it is true that some people for years had to check the plaque or hood ornament on a GM car to tell a Pontiac from an Oldsmobile. Considerable amounts are invested in market research to determine what symbols prove to be the strongest, most persuasive elements of influence, most pleasing to the eye, most memorable and reflective of the product itself.

The process often looks incredibly simple, as in the case of General Motors (logo: the letters "GM" encased in a rectangle), General Electric (logo: the letters "GE" within a circle) and IBM (logo: the letters "IBM"). Designers and graphic artists will painstakingly explain it's much more complex than that. Dozens of illustrations and techniques are considered before a final selection is made. Countless styles of typeface are evaluated and tested. Indeed, in the case of Xerox (logo: the word "Xerox"), an original typeface was created.

A story destined to become a part of corporate identity folklore has the National Broadcasting Company—NBC— wanting to replace the colorful "Peacock" logo with something more crisp and contemporary. After a fair amount of time and cost reported to be around $750 thousand, the network proudly revealed its new symbol, a letter "N." Public reaction was a chortle, which turned into a hoarse laugh when a Nebraska public television station announced they were there first, with a strikingly similar letter "N" as their logo, created at a cost of a few hundred dollars. A little more research, a little more creativity, a little less fanfare could have saved a lot of embarrassment.

While the basic function of the logo is to simply identify the product or company and help it stand out from the competition, psychological influences are significant. Often, it is not just a symbol that's involved, it's *symbolism.* The Dreyfus lion and the Merrill Lynch bull are two examples of attempts to infer power, strength, and dominance among peers—what could even be described as the suggestion of animal magnetism. All this from a symbol, without yet revealing the product name.

But that's the *essence* of the logo. When it succeeds, it identifies without showing its name. While it is true that some companies use a distinctive typeface and design *as* their logo, others tell you who you're watching or dealing with by sign, not syllable:

➠ The winged horse identifies Mobil Oil

➠ The winged shoe identifies Goodyear

- The torch on a shield says Amoco
- A "T" in a star in a circle is Texaco
- Golden arches say McDonald's
- A little girl, holding an umbrella, walking in the rain, is Morton Salt
- An eye suggests CBS
- A rock means Prudential

These companies have done a powerfully effective job of so permeating people's consciousness that their symbol—especially when viewed outside common items such as caps, jackets, key chains, canvas bags, coffee mugs, towels or other promotional devices—make one think of the company or product. The continued visibility over time was critical.

Some companies have it easy when it comes to creating or adapting a logo. Unfortunately, not all of us have companies called Green Giant or Arm & Hammer. But logos tend to change with the current fashion. For a time, the marketplace will seem to be buried in symbols of waves, pentagons, arcs, and swirls; as the cycle changes, see these logos replaced by the company or the product name in simple, understated type. Columbia Records, Chrysler, and RCA are the companies with an almost predictable cycle of understated-to-overstated-and-back-again corporate graphics.

Acronyms identifying a company or product by the first letters of its name is a kind of visual and verbal shorthand that presumes the marketplace knows a company by either or both its name and initials. If the marketplace guesses wrong, the identity suffers, perhaps twice. If the company succeeds, one might say they are twice as well-known.

The following are some products or companies known as well by their initials as by name—sometimes better:

AAA	GM	MCI
A&P	GMAC	MGM
AT&T	GTE	NCR
A&W	IBM	RCA
BASF	IDS	STP
BMW	ITT	TRW
GAF	JVC	TWA
GE	MCA	

Al Ries and Jack Trout in their book *Positioning: The Battle for your Mind* discourage the dependency on corporate or product acronyms, a process they call "the no-name trap."

They note a number of companies "go to a lot of trouble making sure [their] name looks right without considering how it sounds. "True enough. People are sensitive to both sound and sight. Your name, logo and signature, on items from products to ads to trucks and balloons, should both look and sound right. We'll call one city L.A., but another is never called N.Y. It just doesn't sound right. Corporate shorthand is fine in internal memos and reports, but the best way to let the public know and become familiar with a company or product name is to *use* that name as much as possible.

The Corporate Identity Program

In many respects, a corporate identity program is like a dress code—defined, inflexible, and rich in symbolism. Some companies, like individuals, take great pride in their names and do not grant others the right to shorten, change, or misuse them. Just as some Roberts prefer not to be called Bob, businesses go to great lengths to protect and control the use of their names. The premise, of course, is totally legitimate and honorable, particularly in instances where a great investment has been advanced in research, focus groups, graphic arts, and advertising. Editorially, control is virtually impossible. However much it might have wished to do so, American Telephone and Telegraph could never stop a writer from referring to it as Ma Bell, and Howard Johnson's Motor Lodge could not avoid HoJo.

When it comes to companies themselves, their various divisions, their advertising agencies, public relations agencies, or anyone who wishes to use a trademarked name in signage, endorsement or other form, the company can and does typically exercise control. Usually this is quite appropriate. Such requirements as indicating trademark, registration, patent, or copyright are correct. To insist that the name be used as intended, which is to say not hyphenated, broken or modified, is certainly appropriate. Many companies having invested heavily in establishing corporate colors, may require that when a logo or signature be represented in color, it be in the designated PMS or corporate color. It's even understandable to say that when one logo is used among others, a particular placement position be agreed on and a size ratio specified. Understandably, in work such as this, if Coke's logo were to be shown in the same space as that of Pepsi, or Hyatt along with Hilton, the companies would reserve the right not to be upstaged by their competitors.

An appropriate checklist for the correct use of a company name, logo, and signature can probably be represented in a page or two. Many companies having spent large sums on development of a corporate identity program, apparently believe they haven't gotten their money's worth if they don't have a thick volume (The Corporate Identity Manual) to cap it off. The design firm too often finds this a help in justifying inflated fees. Before designers toss this book in the fire, let's reach an understanding: a talented designer should charge a fee as much as the client is willing to pay. Designers sell talent, skill, and experience.

Experience has shown that after determining size, color, placement, and legal requirements, most all else in these manuals is of dubious value, so they don't get used much. Save a tree, save a forest, skip the manual and keep the requirements for the use of your name simple. Businesses should want the exposure that leads to greater awareness to usage to loyalty to brand equity. Ridiculous restrictions discourage such widespread use.

Name Changes, Mergers, Joint Ventures

"Change for the sake of change" is a pretty worthless idea. Businesses should not do something without a reason. Sometimes the reason is that management feels the company needs a face-lift, a little repositioning, a little more contemporary look and feel about it. After all, it's been years since—

➠ Wait!!

➠ Stop and listen to yourself!

➠ Is the market share holding steady or declining?

➠ Is the competition wiping your nose in every town?

➠ How are profits?

➠ Are customers, retailers, wholesalers, and stock-holders satisfied?

Check your research data (or commission more current research) and analyze it carefully.

Usually, a new manager or management team will want to put their own stamp on things, as the old expression goes. That's fine if it stops at rearranging the furniture, but for something as dramatic as changing a product or company name, one in which much has been invested, be careful.

The Campbell Soup Company has had the same basic, unexciting red and white can for years. And the name and logo is largely the same as it's been. As new varieties are introduced, consumers often have to squint looking for the little "new" snipe on the label. But it's worth it. People have come to trust the quality and consistency of this product over the years and if one day the soup cans were all green and gold with the faces of rock stars on the label, it would be confusing, costly, and would, without a doubt, diminish the product. Obviously, it would also be unnecessary and simply a change for the sake of change.

Do some research and act on its findings. If it tells you you're doing fine, say thank you and get back to work. New management, new marketers, the new ad agency should have an arsenal of creative weapons available to maintain that fresh, competitive energy. Let the creative marketers do their jobs without breaking something that's working fine.

Be suspicious of those who try to "shake things up" without a clear reason. This style of management exists, though no one seems to be able to say why. Remember too that because a new CEO or marketing chief doesn't like a name doesn't mean it's a bad name. Check the research and confirm or disprove.

Sometimes, of course, the need for change is obvious and doesn't have to wait for the research to reveal it.

S. S. Kresge, for example, was doing all right as a neighborhood five-and-ten-cents store in the tradition of F. W. Woolworth. But when Kresge's married the idea of the supermarket to that of the discount department store—shopping carts, product sampling, and instant in-store sales and specials on products from coats to tires to candy canes with plenty of free parking—business exploded. K-Mart was thus born. the new program was so successful that the parent took the child's name and all of Kresge became K-Mart.

When Nash became American Motors, sales continued to fall. When the company even tried changing its name to its biggest selling product, Rambler, sales still dropped. The car just wasn't good enough to compete regardless of its name. Occasionally, even marketers have to be reminded that whatever the name or the ad campaign, it still takes a *product* to succeed.

Research reports told Montgomery Ward Department Stores that stereo systems and other electronic equipment such as answering machines and video recorders were being bought by people younger than their typical customers and that those shoppers wanted more than just a "record player." They wanted the most technically advanced products on the market, prompting the company to create a store-within-the-store: "Electric Avenue." With its own identity, budget, and ad campaign, the venture became very successful. Noteworthy was how it maintained a hot, youthful image very different from that of Montgomery Ward—the middle class, mainstream department store that gave it birth. The residual effect to the parent was that many younger shoppers gave Wards a second look. The company appealed to the younger target group without alienating its core constituency.

In another example, a giant Japanese automaker had global marketing reasons for changing its popular Datsun to Nissan. The transition went so smoothly because it was a non-domestic company. That is to suggest that while Americans had a certain level of familiarity with Datsun, there were also a significant number of new foreign companies on the scene and to take a closer look at the Nissan amid the growing group of imports didn't seem like too much to ask. A U.S. automaker would have had to go considerably further as if, for instance, Ford decided to change the name of its Mercury division to that of perhaps another planet. Established American brands have an institution-like quality few foreign competitors can claim in this market yet.

AYDS reducing candies and wafers came on the market a generation before the tragic and fatal disease was dubbed "AIDS" by medical researchers. A new name and reintroduction would have been in order. Instead, the company left the brand to languish and disappear.

Sometimes after a name change has been decided, there is a tendency to want to put "formerly . . ." under the new name. Let it go. Focus on now and the future.

Merging companies represent a minor challenge. If the names fit comfortably together, use them with a slash, hyphen, comma, or space. If they don't flow nicely enough, the larger, better-known brand should survive to carry the flag. If agreement can't be reached, arrive at the settlement on a neutral name and commission a terrific ad campaign to make sure everyone knows about it. Sometimes in mergers and acquisitions such decisions are dictated by the dreaded legal department. As egos and golden parachutes begin to unfurl, remember that all the rules for naming the product or company still apply. If research tells you that consumers, retailers, and stockholders like it, it's good. If the name is a vanity decision, it could be an expensive one.

When Chrysler Corporation took over the failing American Motors, the latter company was in such sad shape, there was little point—or value to anyone—in keeping the name alive. The respectable models, Jeep and Eagle, were simply brought out the next model year as products of Chrysler.

The pairings of two respected Hollywood logos, Metro-Goldwyn-Mayer and United Artists resulted in "MGM-UA," a lackluster name that faded from view as quickly as the product it produced.

The rule regarding joint ventures is that there are no rules. Normally, with or without a new designation, the line "a joint venture of . . ." allows the opportunity to capitalize on whatever currency has been created in the venture partners individually. The suggestion is of strength through the combining of strong component parts.

Recognize the value and power, indeed the critical importance, of having the right name for your brand. It is often how people determine at a glance or a sound, in a matter of seconds, how they feel about a brand forever.

Choose a name or change to a name that distinguishes you from the pack in the most favorable possible way. In an ad-heavy, information-heavy environment, few choices you will make say so much or carry such currency over time as that of your brand name. Choose carefully.

Protect Yourself

While choice is important and making the wrong choice could hurt the product's chances of success, sometimes the process can be unexpectedly costly, if your plans are stalled, altered, or halted because of a contested name. Every year the courts hear cases of name and trademark infringement. These cases are often both brought by, and defended by, some of America's largest corporations, the folks one would think would be so big and thorough as to be above all that.

It is as important to legally protect a name as it is to create one. Henri Charmasson, a consultant in such matters, offers that

> A good name to identify a company or distinguish its products from others must be unique and original, yet capable of carrying a favorable message to motivate the customer to have dealings with that company. Creating such a name is an art as well as a science with rules and guidelines rooted in sociology, psychology, semantics, and at last but not least, the law.
>
> Commercial names such as *Super Glue* for an adhesive, *Reader* for a newspaper, *Lite* for a low calorie beer and *Windsurfer* for a sailboat . . . are examples of names that courts found to be unworthy of legal protection and have been freely copied as a result.

Some other examples of names that companies tried to own, but were ruled too generic to register, include *air shuttle* for short route airline service, *builders emporium* for a building supply store, *computer merchant, computer store,* and *consumer electronics* as the respective purveyors of the items named. *Dial-a-ride* for ground surface taxi shuttle service, and *safari* for an outlet that would carry, not surprisingly, safari gear. Obviously, the limitations of name ownership extend to the services noted. For example, one might trademark *Safari* for a restaurant or nightclub with a special theme or menu and likely be granted exclusivity. As in the case of "The Computer Store," one can picture the excited marketer thinking how great it would be to have a name that was so obvious and all-encompassing, it would seem like the generic designation of the industry. Alas, the courts agreed . . . and wouldn't let them have it.

An important consideration in building a successful brand name is to be distinctive. A generic-sounding name is little help in defining your brand's personality.

Review

1. Choose a name for the company, product, or service that suggests strength, bigness, stability, has a pleasant look and sound, is not too long or difficult to remember and suggests what the company is or does.

2. Try to put a benefit in the name. *Easy, quick, fresh, safe, rapid, instant,* and *sure* are examples of words used in brand names to suggest benefits.

3. Rely on research to confirm or test your decisions.

4. Let decisions regarding the closeness or distancing from a corporate parent be determined by what *benefits* accrue to each. If they have no reason to be mentioned or linked except to please the board of directors or stock analysts, save underlining the association for the annual report. Remember that people's dislike of a parent company can be passed along as easily as people's likes.

5. Address different audiences differently. Consumers and retailers want benefits to *them*. Don't burden nonprofessionals with information about trademarks, patents, and parent companies.

6. Logos and signatures should be bright, upbeat, and representative of the company or product.

7. Avoid the acronym game. Use names and words that suggest a company or product's pride, spirit, and a benefit.

8. Avoid generating volumes on the use and restrictions of your name and logo. A simple suggestion of size, colors, placement, and trademark protection is enough. Don't create a thick manual that no one will read or use.

9. Rely on research reports, sales figures, profit and loss statements and other feedback from your customers and constituents to tell you if your name still "works"—if it has value in the marketplace. If it doesn't, it might be time for a change in any of a number of forms—from a fresh start or repositioning to a "new and improved" version.

10. Avoid making changes just to *appear* fresh and exciting. React to your market and change only if and when you need to do so.

11. Think of a company name or a product name as having every bit as much the suggestion of pride and good origins as the best "family names." Such names are passed on with a great sense of tradition to future generations.

12. As your name should show your own individuality, try to include a suggestion of some point that differentiates you from your competition. Words like *best, top, just,* and *only* are some that historically have tried to set products apart with a suggestion of uniqueness and superiority.

13. Protect your name legally. Name and trademark challenges are costly and result in negative public relations.

14. Avoid adopting generic-sounding names that lack creativity and probably won't prevail in a legal challenge.

Chapter Two

BUILDING BRAND EQUITY: THE ANATOMY OF A BRAND

*"Never eat anything whose listed ingredients
cover more than one-third of the package."*

— Joseph Leonard

Creating a Brand

The assumption is that by this time the product or service exists and that it has a name. We assume too, you've secured the appropriate trademark protection. The next step is to turn that name into a *brand* by infusing it with a suggestion of value. The difference between simply a name and a brand name is that while a name is an identifying designation, the brand name adds to that a sense of definition and personality.

Professor John Philip Jones of Syracuse University, drawing upon his 25 years in advertising, wrote "A brand is a product that provides functional benefits plus added values that some consumers value enough to buy."

Professor David A. Aaker of the University of California at Berkeley, however, goes a step and several words further, suggesting, "A brand is a distinguishing name and/or symbol (such as a logo, trademark, or package design) intended to identify the goods or services of either one seller or a group of sellers, and to differentiate those goods or services from those of competitors."

Whew!

While neither professor is likely to make it as an ad copywriter, the point should be clear enough: Brands are names and symbols of what they represent.

Now that we have brought a brand into existence, the marketer's role is to bring it into the marketplace and to the attention of interested parties.

At the risk of sounding like Marketing 101, here are some basic questions and answers:

Why Do People Buy?

Because they need or want what's being offered.

Whether a purchase is a need or a want, why do people choose the brands they choose? What are the buyers' hot buttons?

The answer in diagram form, looks like this:

$$\frac{\text{Price} + \text{Quality} = \text{Value}}{\text{Image}}$$

Historically, the price/quality/value tag was only associated with established brand names. The drill went like this:

If you were a better *known* brand in the minds of consumers, you would be considered a better brand. You would be better known because you would be big. You would be big because you would advertise most, which you would do because you would have a bigger budget, because you would be a bigger operation, because you would sell the most product. You could only do this if you were tops and to be so, you would likely be of the highest quality and priced right. Note that priced right doesn't necessarily mean cheapest. Cheap can be synonymous with shoddy/poor/low-quality. And price without quality does not equal value. Price *with* quality equals value, and value is why people choose one brand over another.

That and image—that "feel good" quality.

When someone buys a Mont Blanc pen or a BMW or an Armani suit or a fine wine or good crystal, the person believes he or she is buying quality at an acceptable (though not necessarily the cheapest available) price and getting with it a feeling of taste, style, accomplishment, and yes, status. That's what the higher priced brands sell—status or, just as important, the perception of status.

K-Mart stores offer women's clothing from the Jaclyn Smith collection. These fashions carrying the actress/model's name and endorsement promise taste and style at a fraction of the cost of top name European or New York designers.

Image is a major factor in the buying decision and sometimes it has to do with not only the image to which one aspires (or daydreams), but to one that's a sort of creed.

A person who believes no car should cost as much as a house would not buy an expensive car under any circumstances. Some people will never pay to fly first class whether they can afford it or not.

People will claim they bought cars for a whole host of reasons from good mileage to economy to resale value— every reason except the one the researchers feel is near the top of the list; image, that desire, for example, to slide behind the wheel and feel, for a few minutes, like James Bond.

But while the perception of price/quality/value (and image) was long identified with established brands, modern marketing techniques and technology have combined to render that idea obsolete.

"Instant" Brand Building

Technology gets blamed for a lot. In addition to speed and accuracy, the computer has brought us a new list of excuses for things going wrong—or not going at all (the system is down; we're not programmed for what you want; our system isn't compatible with your system; and the latest and best: we must have a computer virus).

But, for all the excuses, technology and technologists with their laser-like vision have created a world of instant communications.

Marketers had spent years creating brand identification and recognition and building brand loyalty, only to be overshadowed by instant brand-building in the second half of the twentieth century.

In the 1950s, when Arthur Godfrey told television and radio audiences he was pausing for a cup of Lipton Tea, America put the kettle on with him; Lipton outsold its competition, virtually owning the market.

When Paul Harvey told his national radio audiences about "the Gold Book" from Banker's Life, Americans did the unthinkable. They actually called and asked to speak to a life insurance salesman.

In the 1960s, Dick Clark told millions of teenagers watching TV's "American Bandstand" that Beechnut Spearmint gum was "flavorific" and the product virtually sold out coast to coast overnight. It became instantly the brand of choice of America's youth.

But the power of instant brand building reached new heights when, in the 1980s, the fledgling Apple Computer and the little-known Nike footwear spent virtually their entire advertising budget to run one-minute commercials on the Super Bowl game. These commercials would be talked about for months—free—on radio and TV talk shows and certainly on subways and commuter trains across America.

Consumers constantly complain about the glut of advertising—there's too much of it; it's intrusive, insulting, demeaning, and mindless, especially on television.

Yet when:

➠ A blonde Swedish model intoned "All my men wear English Leather . . . or nothing at all . . ."

➠ And when model Brooke Shields squeezed into tight jeans and insisted "Nothing comes between me and my Calvins".

➠ And the beautiful spokeswoman looked at the man with his face covered in shaving cream lather and begged him "take it off - take it all off!"

. . . people stopped what they were doing time and again and watched. More importantly, they bought the products and sales soared.

The common thread in these three examples is the subtle (that is to say, not graphic) use of sex. This is not totally an original idea in advertising. However true it is that sex sells, some ads have also used sexy models and pitches and have fallen flat. The technology may have provided the medium and the medium provided the audience, but bad advertising still annoys and disturbs people and usually doesn't work. Good advertising, on the other hand, works very well—even amid the glut. A single TV commercial, seen often, can create a level of interest that establishes a brand permanently.

McDonald's may always be the fast food leader, but for a while the Golden Arches team had to endure the results of another instant brand success. Wendy's had been around for several years and had been regarded as an okay place for hamburgers, but not an especially hot property. But when the company ran a TV spot with an 80-something-year-old, foggy-voiced woman asking "Where's the beef?" sales sky-rocketed. The line became a part of the culture. Comedians and politicians repeated it on stages coast to coast, each time giving, in effect, free advertising by conjuring up the memo-ries of Wendy's and of overnight star Clara Peller.

In the late 1980s, as a health conscious America loaded up on exercise videos, cassettes, and club memberships, one television commercial, inexpensively produced, ran in off-hours, off-network and sold millions of the "Thighmaster" exercise device worldwide.

Calvin Klein's Obsession cologne flew off the shelves in weeks because of a few artfully developed, immensely crea-tive, beautifully photographed television and print ads that suggested fears, fantasies, dreams—anything but fragrance. The ads became the subject of much conversation and con-troversy. Successes such as this previously took years, not weeks.

Advertising Creates Awareness

There are other ways to generate awareness, certainly some less expensive than TV advertising. But when it comes to presenting your message, controlling the timing, space, con-tent, and the number of times and places the message is viewed by a fairly scientifically determined demographic target, advertising in general—and TV advertising in particular—continues to be the most effective method. Consider too that, while both were considered instant successes, the Thighmaster ads, in terms of both production and media, cost a fraction of what the Calvin Klein Obsession ads cost. Instant success doesn't have to cost millions. Consider this:

➠ Advertising creates awareness

➠ There is a measurable relationship between level of awareness and share of market

This repeats the belief that if yours is a *better known* brand, it is a *better* brand.

Brand equity is the value or the perception of value in the brand name. Establishing that value begins with creating awareness. There are two ways to do this: quickly or slowly.

The slow process, which some might argue is more likely to achieve lasting results, involves the following steps:

1. *Going market by market* or city to city to introduce the product to
   a. test groups
   b. influential persons or groups who will endorse or otherwise raise the level awareness through word-of-mouth advertising

2. *Sampling*—distributing free product samples (or free trial service) to targeted groups, again, on a market-by-market basis

3. *Advertising*—As a step in the process or as an option, media advertising (print, television, radio, outdoor) or point-of-sale displays and promotions, is a fairly traditional approach. What is *not* traditional in the most effective programs is the creativity involved in both the media plan and the ads

themselves. There is "awareness advertising" that lets or makes the public know the product exists, and there is "image advertising" that influences how the public views the product. Either approach can be powerful and memorable with the right creative treatment. The media plan—where and how often the work is presented—can include safe, solid, effective mainstream placements or unusual outlets that, while riskier, often gain greater attention.

4. *Sponsorships*—the possibilities are almost endless: TV shows, art exhibits (fine arts to pop art), student competitions (Little League to scholarship grants), concerts, or sporting events from tournaments to marathons.

5. *Promotions—an area that has come of age.* Once this meant putting your name or logo on pens and key rings. It's still that—plus clothing, jewelry, and other premiums—but it's also tie-ins with books, movies, events, and other products to maximize budgets and visibility.

6. *Public relations*—generating awareness through non-paid media such as TV and radio interviews, call-in or lifestyle shows; placement of stories and articles; expositions and announcements.

7. *Event or cause participation*—a little P. R., a little sponsorship, a lot of recognition, visibility, and awareness. Subsidies, endowments, and grants— the support of a school, charity, or other worthy cause—have long been subtle, but effective methods of creating loyalty.

8. *Endorsements*—recognition by an independent research or testing organization often separates

products and emphasizes quality: Approved by Underwriters Laboratories; the Good Housekeeping Seal of Approval; approved and recommended by nine out of ten doctors, etc.

The *quick* way to achieve awareness is to do all of the above listed steps, only more quickly. Critics describe this process as *hype*. While the slow process, step by step and market by market, might be completed over a period of years (a three-to-five-year test and phase-in is not unusual), the fast alternative might be to accomplish steps one through eight in months, or perhaps even in a single high-profile event (the impact of which would linger and result in substantial word-of-mouth advertising).

A number of brands have benefitted from the slow, methodical process of program sponsorship, building a star-quality brand.

Hallmark Hall of Fame	Kraft Theater
Texaco Star Theater	Kraft Music Hall
Colgate Comedy Hour	The Chevy Show
Alcoa Presents	U.S. Steel Hour
Voice of Firestone	Chrysler Playhouse
Ford Theater	Camel News Caravan

Years ago, the fast-break hype approach was a flashy route and not practiced often. The slower market-by-market alternative allowed for gauging public response and, if necessary, making adjustments or even major changes before moving on. Sometimes, of course, if a product fared badly in initial markets, it might well never see national release, a sort of limit-the-losses approach.

Yes, the fast approach—doing everything at once—cost a lot more than inching your way along and paying as you go. The rationale, however, is that, if you believe you're likely to implement the full program over time anyway, whether the reasons have to do with faith or commitment, there are economies of scale to making deals and power buying. Skilled media planners, knowing the cost of buying individual markets, can make national and network buys, reaching those same markets for a fraction of the cost per market of the local buys. Simply put, a major time or space buy has more leverage and power than a minor local buy.

Additionally, there are often enormous research, development and other start-up costs involved, and investors frequently want evidence quickly that a product is on the right track. A big splash tends to get a fairly immediate response. Further, there is often a concern about market dominance. If the product is introduced in small or secondary markets and methodically evaluated—and well received—a possibility always exists that a larger, well capitalized competitor could rush a similar product into the wider marketplace. This makes the original product look as if *it* is the imitator and second best. So the major fast break is a preemptive strike, getting there first and staking a claim.

Which introduces the second reason to consider this alternative: when you're *not* first.

Your product may be in development or even still in the idea stage and a competitor launches a similar or virtually identical product. Coincidence? Conspiracy? Industrial espionage? For purpose of this example, the reason doesn't matter. All that matters is regardless of whether your product is better, someone else is out there first, getting consumers to test and tell about it. It is at such moments as this that colorful slogans such as "You tried the rest, now try the best" are born. If you have to play catch-up, the slower approach won't do. The faster approach will likely even need to be expanded to include enhancements such as celebrity spokespersons/endorsers, discount coupons, and perhaps a contest or sweepstakes. It's full speed ahead to not just catch up, but overtake the other brand.

One example of this race was the wine cooler market of the 1980s. Basically a reintroduction of the "pop wines" of the '60s and '70s (Boone's Farm, Annie Greensprings, etc.), the wine cooler beverage mixed wine with soda in individual serving bottles and sold in four-packs or six-packs. The first major advertising was for the California Cooler, and it was an instant hit. Gallo wineries came second with their Bartles & Jaymes brand. A clever and hugely popular television ad campaign supported by high profile print and in-store displays and a substantial advertising budget was key to the second brand rapidly becoming the category leader. Alas, by the time Seagrams, another giant in the spirits industry, entered the cooler business, even its major Hollywood movie stars, signed for seven-figure endorsement deals, couldn't catch up to Bartles & Jaymes. The brand remained number one until the category fizzled in 1990, a product whose time had come and gone. Again.

There are a number of companies that have chosen to augment their name recognition by sponsoring non-media events. The advantages of such an approach are increasing name recognition and positive image building. These events give the appearance that the sponsor is not interested in selling product, but in furthering an event for the "common good"; a sort of "community service" with some invisible strings attached. Some examples of companies that used alternative non-media sponsorships to help in building star-quality brands are:

The Kemper Open	Volvo Tennis
Virginia Slims Open	Marlboro Grand Prix
The Firestone 500	Tour d'Trump
Bud (Budweiser) Triathalon	
Philip Morris Bill of Rights Traveling Exhibit	

Positioning the Brand

A popularly overused and sometime confused word in modern marketing is *positioning*. Al Ries and Jack Trout used it in a 1981 book, describing it as "a new approach to communication." They offered that positioning is not something a company does with the product, but something that takes place in the mind of the prospect for that product.

Professor David Aaker believes that "Positioning is closely related to the association and image concepts except that it implies a frame of reference, the reference point usually being competition."

When marketers speak of positioning a product, it is generally assumed they mean all of that and perhaps more. To position a product can mean to attempt to conjure an image or association in a mental frame of reference or to physically place it in a particular section of a store or make it available through a service where one may expect to find it.

For example, items or an entire line of clothing sold in a shop located in a fine hotel may suggest clothing for the traveler who suddenly finds himself or herself in need of something inadvertently left at home or unexpectedly needed for a function. However, an upscale hotel would by intention not carry a low-priced or medium-priced item or line of clothing, as it would not be in keeping with the hotel's own image, much less that of the guests who would choose such a hotel. Thus, the brand of clothing would be "positioned" as being a particular level of quality. Of course, the customer assumes a certain higher price reflects the convenience of availability, but assumes too that a fine hotel would not carry a line that wasn't up to its own quality standard.

Vitamins and other nutritional supplements that are only sold through health food stores or fitness centers distinguish—or position—themselves against brands that are mass marketed (usually at a much lower price) in drug stores, supermarkets, or discount chain stores. The location or business itself and the physical placement of the product within that type of environment makes a strong statement to consumers about how they should regard this product relative to the competition. The product whose advertising or label includes the phrase "sold only in fine specialty stores" is trying to raise the suggested level of quality of the product without even addressing it. The implication is that there is something different, unique, better, or special about the product because of where the consumer had to go to get it. This is, where applicable, a clever bit of marketing strategy for smaller companies that may lack the resources to mass market the brand even if they wanted to.

In a much larger sense, positioning is at the very center of creating and building brand equity. If brand equity is the perceived value of the product—how people think of the product or service on its own and relative to the competition—then that perceived valve basically describes the "position" in their minds. Getting the product to that point, of course, is one of the marketer's great challenges.

Thinking of positioning in this sense takes us back to the process of creating awareness. In defining the difference between "image advertising" and "corporate advertising," we note that corporate advertising's goal is awareness, *making people think of the brand*. Image advertising tries to influence *how* they think of the brand. Defining the brand with imagery is a shortcut to building brand awareness and value.

For years, Wheaties breakfast cereal called itself the "Breakfast of Champions" and often featured an illustration of a sports figure on the package. Manufacturer General Mills seemed content to ignore the daydreams of the little girls who wanted to be doctors or teachers or boys who hoped to become judges or architects. In those three words, "Breakfast of Champions," Wheaties spoke volumes of ad copy to the football, baseball, basketball, soccer, swimming, tennis, volleyball, and skating stars of tomorrow, which they were assuming took in most kids.

The simplicity of the Apple computer ads, emphasizing terms like "user-friendly," told the nervous non technical types there was not only nothing to fear, but this thing was actually *friendly*.

Note that positioning a product is not the same as advertising it. "Breakfast of Champions," for example, appeared in the ads, but on the packaging, and in promotions, it was a "positioning statement," to a degree, used to differentiate the brand from other popular brands in its category, such as chief rivals Kellogg's Corn Flakes, Cheerios, and Post Raisin Bran.

Advertising is one, perhaps the most inclusively effective, component of the marketing plan utilized to *achieve* positioning. It is typically within advertising that the positioning strategies of associating the product with imagery pleasing to the consumer can be accomplished, as well as clearly differentiating the product from its competition. Promotions, special events, sponsorships, and publicity are all excellent tactics for raising the level of awareness but typically do not lend themselves to the kind of competitive differentiation so important to staking out a product's position in the marketplace. This differentiation can be mapped out in the marketing plan.

Marketing Plan

No product, regardless of how large or small the company, should be brought to market without a well-defined *marketing plan*. Your marketing plan may be as different as you are from your competition. Like the corporate identity manual, marketing plans may be a single-page checklist or a thick volume. and like other manuals, the thicker they are, the less likely they are to be used.

Your marketing plan is your basic road map, laying out the tone, pace, direction, parameters, and cost of getting where you want to go. It should be realistic in terms of goals and budgets. Typically, the plan follows an outline like the following:

I. **Situation Analysis**
    A. Your own position
    B. Your competition
    C. Government and regulatory environment
    D. Public attitudes toward your product, your company, and your competition

II. **Objectives**
    A. Your overall goal in terms of sales, market share, changes in attitudes, and awareness
    B. Timetable for achieving your objective(s)

III. **Strategy**
    A. To some, a marketing plan represents a strategy in and of itself. This defines your approach to meeting your objectives.

IV. **Tactics**
    A. The approach to implementing your strategy: advertising, publicity, promotions, lobbying—any or all.

V. **Evaluation**
    A. Benchmarks for achieving your objectives
    B. Revision, as needed, to strategy and tactics

Above and below each of these points is the issue of budget. Goals should not only be realistic in terms of their creative ability to be met, but in your ability to fund the strategy and tactics to achieve them. To that end, your marketing plan should also be flexible.

University of Tulsa Marketing Professor Robert D. Hisrich notes that "In order to carry out effective planning and control, managers must have relevant and accurate information on a continual basis." The relevant and accurate information to which he is referring is *research*, an essential component of every marketing plan.

Again, it doesn't matter how large or small the company is—or the goals of the brand—going into the marketplace without a plan that includes research is like flying without radar. You might get there, but do you really want to insist on maximizing your risks?

Some companies spend enormous amounts on detailed research such as multi-page questionnaires, phone surveys, focus groups, and demographic and/or psychographic studies. Others merely compile some data—usually in the form of opinions—from a random or selected group of customers, dealers, or sales reps. Somewhere in between is probably the correct approach for most companies. Most major business and trade publications have considerable market research data on file which they are usually delighted to share with their advertisers. A typical issue of a magazine such as *American Demographics* offers information on trends and buying habits that once cost thousands of dollars to compile. Other research operations have newsletters and studies available on almost any subject.

However one acquires it, reliable research information can mean the difference between hitting a target dead on and making costly mistakes. A CEO or manager who dismisses or minimizes the need for research claiming to know his or her market, product, or prospect certainly might be right. But doing business under the best of circumstances carries enough risks and variables. Why add to them?

Before rolling out the brand, determine the following:

1. What is the potential market for the product?

2. Who is your customer?
   a. male/female/both/child/parent/families/ single people/students . . .
   b. income
   c. geographic area or region
   d. education

3. Who/what is your competition?
   a. company
   b. product

4. How are you (company *and* product) perceived relative to your competition?

5. What is the history, if any, of companies, products, or services who have tried before?

6. How great a consideration is the reputation of your company in the minds of the consumer?

7. Does this product complement or compete with another product of your company?

Adding Value to a Brand Name

Exactly what constitutes value is subject to change.

Some companies painstakingly build up their brands over the years through huge advertising and marketing budgets, some by physically positioning themselves conveniently (the corner store, as close as your neighborhood . . .), some through word-of-mouth advertising, and some through the quality of their service or their guarantee.

At least two generations made Sears "where America shops" at least partly because of their guarantee. Buy it at a Sears store in Chicago and, if you're not completely satisfied, return it to a Sears store in Miami, Detroit, or wherever it's most convenient for *you* to do so. The Sears name meant service and value. They were also located in the most heavily populated areas.

Ironically, Sears lost its preeminence as the world's largest retailer to K-Mart and Wal-Mart, two companies *not* in populated areas, but on the outskirts of most major cities. Further, they both put price above service and found that shoppers were willing to drive further, wait in longer checkout lines and accept a manufacturer's guarantee, if one were offered, over the store's own guarantee.

Value clearly did not mean the same thing to everyone. This, again, underscores the need for ongoing research to track trends and public taste shifts as well as changes in priorities. To a certain market segment, the higher price tag of the Cadillac, Lincoln, and BMW will always represent quality and value. They can afford it. But in recessionary times, or when simply watching the family budget, quality and value may have to be redefined. The marketer at this time must decide to

1.　Redefine the target market

2.　Reposition the product

3.　Change the product

4.　Or perhaps all of the above

In some cases, cutting prices can produce the opposite effect of the one desired. When BMW announced that it would introduce a lower priced model for the belt-tightness of the 1990s, public reaction was negative from BMW owners who saw the status and value of their brand being diminished.

When Cadillac saw the trends moving to smaller, more fuel-efficient cars in the 1980s, they sought to move away from the Cadillac "gas guzzler" image with a smaller car. It flopped. Cadillac owners wanted luxury and status, not just another choice in the crowded field of compacts.

How might these two auto giants have responded differently?

One way would have been to conduct research among their *current* customers, rather than among prospective customers. A certain respect for the consumer is displayed when a company is able to introduce a new line with phrases like "you asked for it" or "you told us what you wanted in a luxury car." Enhancing the value of a service package, a warranty, or a trade-in or upgrade option adds value without diminishing the perception of quality. When Volvo cited the number of years their cars were on the road (more than the average person assumed), the message was that their cars were worth the extra money. Showing the savings in replacement parts as compared to a lesser product is another way of saying that lower price doesn't always mean value.

Research must tell you not just what trends are affecting your customers, but help you keep your finger on their pulse. Do they define such terms as quality, convenience, service, and value as they did when you conducted your first survey? Tastes change. Monitoring customer satisfaction is as important as initially defining your target.

Airline mileage points, cash rebates from the Discover card, merchandise checks from the GE Rewards Visa card, a replacement guarantee for the items purchased with an American Express card, extra time to pay on a revolving charge card, and lower financing rates have all replaced the value-added concept of Blue Chip and S & H Green Stamps of years ago. It is not a new discovery that even the most upscale customers appreciate getting more for their money. Companies and products that last consistently strive to give more—or at least the *perception* of giving more.

This is not to suggest deceiving the customer, but remember that much of what has been outlined in this section—the use of images, associations, and differentiation—represents both practical distinctions and emotional distinctions. Making people feel good about a product is defined as added value. Perhaps they feel good because they've saved money on the giant economy size or because the product is good for the environment or because a percentage of the manufacturer's profits benefit the Special Olympics. People will often choose a brand for intangible reasons, especially if the right message guides them to do so. There is nothing deceptive in finding and exploiting value in the brand or how it is marketed.

Brand Distribution

It might seem as though a discussion of distribution should be about *product* distribution and, of course, it is. But consider how certain lines—Amway, Avon, Mary Kay, Shaklee, and NuSkin, to name a few—distribute their products exclusively through direct home sales, typically via multi-level marketing groups.

Indeed, part of their very appeal is that this is the *only* way one can buy their products. In that respect, brand distribution becomes a part of brand building. Other names, such as Ronco, and K-tel, built their reputations by selling a myriad of products through "exclusive TV offers." True, this is advertising, not distribution per se, but it suggests a limited accessibility, an exclusivity.

The 1980s phenomenon of the "infomercial," program-length television commercials, offered reading programs, real estate courses, makeup and hair care products, and diet plans only available "for a limited time . . . and only from this 800 number."

The Body Shop's well-regarded line of personal care products (in that the company founders are high profile environmentalists) are only available from their chain of franchised and company-owned stores around the world. Again, part of the marketing message, or mystique, is the exclusivity of the distribution method.

Other enterprises, such as Victoria's Secret, Land's End, and L. L. Bean offer their branded merchandise in a limited number of stores bearing their names, but mainly sell to catalog shoppers, an enormous and growing market segment.

Under normal circumstances, distribution is a major factor in brand building. That is, historically if a product could be sold through a major chain store, its very presence represented a certain assumed or perceived level of integrity, acceptance, and quality. Additionally, the *volume* of product sold was large because the chain itself was large. The exposure on such a wide scale made a difference.

We use the expression "under normal circumstances" because what is normal is as changeable as market conditions. Products like the Thighmaster or the Juice King, or the Veg-o-Matic, or Deal-A-Meal weight loss program would have had to spend months with large colorful displays and bright packaging blocking the aisles of Wal-Mart, K-Mart, and Macy's stores before any profit would have been in sight. But a series of 60-second television spots scattered across the country during the cheapest times of day on secondary (or less) TV stations sold millions of units, often without even an inventory being maintained.

Another broad relationship to distribution is telemarketing, an area that continues to draw the public's wrath. Complaints constantly pour into the regulatory agencies, consumer advocate organizations, and the media, about the intrusive phone calls that interrupt dinner, naps, and life itself. Yet enormous sales numbers accrue in products as diverse as magazine subscriptions, season theater tickets, imported wines, and credit card insurance. While the process of telemarketing is a sales process, the product is being marketed with a form of brand distribution exclusivity.

Despite criticism of multi-level marketing operations as "pyramids" and frauds, there are still few methods of generating interest, awareness, and sales as effective as the word-of-mouth announcement and endorsement from a neighbor or friend—who always remembers to ask for the order, as well as the names of other people to call.

In the 1970s unrequested postal deliveries introducing new products or brands or offering "special low discount prices for buying direct" were usually addressed to the "occupant" at your address. This was called "junk mail." By the 1980s, however, such mailings had evolved to carefully and scientifically developed lists, based on demographic and psychographic data. These mailings were the foundation of what had come to be called "direct marketing," which for several years was the darling of the advertising industry as a targeted alternative to the traditional media buy.

Typical avenues of distribution have included retail specialty and department stores, discount stores, supermarkets, superstores, and, obviously depending on the products, mail order catalogs, door-to-door sales, and even vending machines.

Now, with new computer technology and cable television, the avenues have widened. Mail and phone lists are more targeted, more accurate, and personalized. TV is more finely tuned, with sports channels and science channels targeting a segmented market for an 800-number tied to a "direct marketing" pitch. Components of the media schedule become distribution outlets and vice versa.

Distribution is as much a function of marketing as it is a function of operations. Think of "brand distribution" as a part of the "brand building" process. Understand that *how* a product is distributed is a major factor in how people relate to it: as either unique and special or as part of a pile of other products. If advertising is supposed to utilize a unique selling proposition to distinguish one brand of product from another, a creative approach to distribution could be both a part of that proposition or the proposition itself.

Review

1. Price and quality equal value. Value, or the perception of value, is why people choose one brand over another. Identify value in your product or service.

2. Image—that *feel good* quality—is an important component of value.

3. There is a measurable relationship between a brand's level of public awareness and its market share.

4. Create and continually fine-tune your Marketing Plan, the road map to a successful program.

5. Position your brand in the right place physically/geographically as well as in the mind of the consumer, both alone and relative to your competition.

6. Clearly differentiate your brand from that of your competition. Find its *unique selling proposition*.

7. Consider creative methods of distribution as part of a brand-building technique.

Building Brand Loyalty

Whatever Became of That Brand?

As each generation comes of age, the term nostalgia takes on a new and important meaning to them. More than ever before, marketers are learning this. The old magazines piled up in the garage for years are now selling at the nostalgia shop for 20 times their cover prices. Tapping the reservoir of warm memories can be very profitable.

One of the most effective ad campaigns for Alka-Seltzer in the late 1980s involved reframing an old black and white TV commercial from some 30 years earlier. Baby boomers sat smiling, watching the animated character "Speedy" come out of retirement and cheerfully sell a lot of pain reliever.

The Nestlé Company brought back a nearly 40-year-old television idea using the puppet dog "Farfel" of ventriloquist Jimmy Nelson. Mr. Nelson still did the off-screen voice, but he no longer appeared in the ads. While the puppet looked the same as audiences remembered, the youthful puppeteer had become eligible for Medicare.

7-Up resumed calling itself "the Uncola" and, after a lengthy absence, despite changing its signature from Kentucky Fried Chicken to the less cholesterol-intensive KFC, the brand remembered to tell its target market "we do chicken right," a theme line of earlier times.

But while some brands, still selling and a part of the landscape, bring a flash of instant recognition and appreciation, others become answers to trivia questions. The March 11, 1957 issue of *Life* magazine featured on its cover a young U. S. Senator, John F. Kennedy. The issue, an accurate mirror of the time, carried within its pages some 125 ads. Among those brands that could still ring familiar more than 35 years later:

Allstate Insurance	Hunt's Tomato Sauce
American Dairy Association	Imperial Margarine
Arrow Shirts	John Hancock Insurance
Bayer Aspirin	Kellogg's Rice Crispies
Betty Crocker Cake Mix	Lipton Tea
Birds Eye frozen vegetables	Lucky Strike cigarettes
Campbell's Soup	Maytag
Canadian Club	Mercury
Carnation Evaporated Milk	No-doz
Chevrolet	Pepsi-Cola
Colgate toothpaste	Pontiac
Diamond Walnuts	Ritz Crackers
Dr. Scholl's Foot Powder	Schick electric razors
Drano	Schlitz beer
Equitable Insurance	Scripto pens
Ford	7-Up
Fruit of the Loom	Smirnoff vodka

Chapter Three

General Electric	Texaco
Glidden paint	Western Union
Hanes stockings	Winston cigarettes

Other ads in the same magazine were for brands that may not be quite so familiar. The products or companies, once popular, have either ceased to exist or have so diminished in market presence that they may as well have ceased to exist. When did anyone last see these bygone brands?

Anzac by House of Worsted-Tex
Bestform girdles and bras
Bluettes and Ebonetts rubber gloves
Duplicolor auto touch-up paint
Esterbrook pens
Evening in Paris deodorant
FoMoCo (Ford automotive replacement parts)
L & M cigarettes
Musterole (pain ointment)
Neuralbaum Liniment
Norcross greeting cards
River Brand Rice
Schrank's Dreamwear
Snow Crop (frozen fruits and vegetables)
Stanback (headache) powders and tablets
Style-Mart Gulftone clothes
Super Anahist cold remedy
Tempo—"the quick mix for meatloaf"
Tru-Glo liquid make-up
Tru Val shirts, sportswear, pajamas
Veto deodorant

Please note that the following major national brands—cars, soaps, and cigarettes—went out without a bang. They just quietly fell from prominence to become footnotes in brand name history.

Acnecare	Hudson cars
American Family Flakes	Instant Postum beverage
American Family Snow	Ipana toothpaste
Beechnut gum	Kaiser-Frazer cars
Bel-Air cigarettes	Num deodorant
Burgess batteries	Nash cars
Candettes Antibiotic Lozenges	Old Gold cigarettes
Chum Gum	Old Nick candy
Clapp's Baby Food	Packard cars
DeSoto cars	Paxton cigarettes
Dr. Lyon's toothpaste and powder	Philip Morris cigarettes
Duz detergent	Raleigh cigarettes
Edsel cars	Rinso detergent
Herbert Tareyton cigarettes	Spring cigarettes
Hit Parade cigarettes	Tip-Top bread
	York cigarettes

Most people can recall a long-gone brand from childhood and ask "Whatever became of . . .?" Was it a lack of advertising or marketing support?

Changing tastes and trends?

A flawed marketing strategy?

Perhaps it was simply a bad product that deserved to die a slow and unnoticed death?

Could the company have been driven out of business by an unscrupulous multi-national conglomerate?

Maybe.

Maybe it was one or all of these reasons, but very likely ongoing market research—taking the pulse of the market—and a plan that anticipated "worst case scenarios" could well have kept these names familiar in contemporary life.

A marketing plan will define, position, and lay out a strategy to build a brand, but often after achieving acceptance and healthy sales, a brand will become a *name brand*, established and successful and sit back while new, aggressively marketed brands knock it not simply off the top, but into oblivion. If that sounds like an overstatement, look again at the list of bygone names. One might assume that a successful brand would never achieve its level of success if its handlers had not been market sensitive. One's second reaction is to remember the first law of business is to "never assume."

But to the matter of survival of the fittest, defined as *strong* as well as *well-capitalized*, it is again a function of a good marketing plan. The plan must provide for not only building brand *awareness*, but brand *loyalty*.

Brand Loyalty

In test markets, beverage manufacturers, for example, know that if people don't like the taste of a product, they won't buy it. Not even *once*. But marketers know too that they can't assume that just because consumers *like* a product and even buy it a few times that they will become regular and loyal customers.

Brand loyalty rarely just happens; you have to make it happen.

These are the exceptions, of course, and sometimes brand loyalty occurs through no effort of the marketer. Sometimes, even when a product is not promoted, it presents an attractive image to a particular cusomer. A would-be novelist admired the work of Kurt Vonnegut and sought to emulate his style. Mr. Vonnegut in his writing made frequent references to his being a heavy smoker of Pall Mall cigarettes. So the admirer became a regular and loyal patron of the brand himself. As much as the marketers of Pall Mall cigarettes in its very best days might have sought to position the brand to win the aspiring writer's attention, their efforts would have been irrelevant. Of course, as an advertising device, the use of celebrity endorsers has proved very successful. In the Vonnegut/Pall Mall example, however, it would have been a case of preaching to the choir. True believers don't have to be sold.

Some Chevrolet owners proudly announce that they represent three generations of Chevy owners. It doesn't much matter where or how the cars are promoted as far as these folks are concerned. "If they were good enough for grandpa and good enough for daddy, then they are . . ."

Well, it usually isn't that easy.

The brand choice is made on the basis of brand image and value (price and quality—or the perception of quality).

The decision to remain loyal to that brand is based on these considerations:

- value (price and quality)
- image (both the brand's own "personality" and its reputation)
- convenience and ease of availability
- satisfaction
- service
- guarantee or warranty

In terms of *value,* long-term use of the brand in one sense suggests loyalty, but much of the responsibility for keeping this going lies in the brand manager or manufacturer.

A lessening of quality standards will disappoint even the most loyal supporters, as will a price change that appears unwarranted. In some cases, it is helpful to advertise the manufacturer's suggested retail price. In instances of an automobile where a dealer will sell a car for less than the suggested price, everyone looks good. In the case of a candy bar where the suggested price is fifty cents, the big chain stores sells it for forty, but the convenience store wants ninety-five, leaving the customer at the latter place to mumble "How can they charge *that* much for this?" At times like that, advertise your price well, and let the retailer explain the "overhead" to the customer. Remember, too, the advantage in publicizing how long you've gone without a price increase, while so much else has gone up (perhaps, including the competitor's brand). Being able to hold the line on price increases your ability to claim value.

Some brands have dealt with the price/value consideration in inflationary times by keeping the price the same and lowering the volume or weight of the product. Others have increased the size or weight as a way to justify a price increase.

The *image* of a company and brand can share a point noted earlier regarding "awareness." As there is a measurable correlation between awareness and market share, so too will there be a connection between a brand's image and market share. Products that are publicized as "environmentally friendly" or "green" build fierce brand loyalty among a growing market segment. Johnson & Johnson's swift handling of the Tylenol product-tampering matter reinforced its reputation as a brand you could trust. Mobil Oil company's sponsorship of artistic endeavors, including Public Television and "Masterpiece Theater" raises its profile as a good corporate citizen, earns goodwill, and builds brand loyalty. The personality a brand takes on is of great importance as in the case of the woman-oriented Virginia Slims cigarettes marketed with the now classic line "You've come a long way, baby." "The Pepsi Generation," "For those who think Young,"and McDonald's "You deserve a break today" were lines that helped define the personality of the brand and build the type of consumer identification—the identifying one's self with the brand—that leads to brand loyalty. Why will some people drive or walk a considerable distance past one service station or fast food restaurant to get to another one? Certainly price and quality are factors, but in most cases the reason the brand is preferred is related to its image; an image the customer has come to identify with.

Convenience and Availability

Convenience and ease of availability can make a difference in brand loyalty. A company may run huge ads touting great sale prices, offer special discounts to students, senior citizens, and people with pets, spend a fortune on mailing coupons and issuing credit cards, but if the location is not convenient (too far away, in an unsafe area, having inadequate parking, not accessible by public transportation), it is doubtful the public will take full advantage of the generosity. In an increasingly stress-filled, demanding society, the brand or company that gets the business is the one that offers products that can be purchased and picked up conveniently, ordered by phone, paid for by credit card, delivered within a reasonable time, and easily returned.

Chapter Three

Satisfaction

Satisfaction is often why Chevy owners remain Chevy owners and why coffee makers, watches, auto parts, and water heaters tend to be replaced with the brand being retired. Satisfaction can be very often defined as the collective embodiment of all the other factors on the brand loyalty checklist (value, image, convenience, service, and guarantee).

Service

Service is one of the most overused words and under-delivered commodities in business today. Several years ago, *Time* ran a cover story with the headline "Why Is Service So Bad?" The same story could have been written at any time several years before or after it appeared. Most surveys reveal that what the customer wants most from his or her bank, dry cleaners, supermarket, lawyer, accountant, shoe repair shop, post office, and restaurant is service. Business has known it for a very long time, promised it in ads and signage, yet seems forever inadequate to the task. The "service window," "service desk" or "customer service" department or phone clerk is where the customer gets told nothing can be done or referred to someone else. Reasons for a high level of dissatisfaction can be traced to overpromising. If you can't service your customers in an efficient, timely and courteous way or train your employees to be courteous, respectful, and responsive to requests or complaints or to deliver, repair, or replace what was offered, don't say that you can. Don't promise a level of service you can't deliver. Just as people will simply not return to a restaurant with good food if they receive bad service, they *will* go back to a restaurant with mediocre food if the service is very good.

Brands that are not measurably better than lower-priced competitors often enjoy repeat business because of quality service.

Guarantee or Warranty

While not everyone takes advantage of a guarantee or warranty, the mere fact that it is offered adds value to a product. When someone does utilize a guarantee, the result is an increase in brand loyalty, particularly when it is then used effectively as an opportunity to gain research information, create a cross-sell or upgrade opportunity.

Brand Loyalty: Case Studies

Cigarettes.   Cigarette smokers offer a good illustration of the unique devotion that is brand loyalty. Smokers will usually stay with the same brand for years without being able to say why. Some will say taste or that a particular brand is less harsh. The occasional smoker will offer that all cigarettes taste pretty much the same; it's questionable if serious smokers could distinguish one brand from another by name in a blind taste test. Such things as freshness and the degree of moisture will alter the qualities of the cigarettes in the same package. If price were a truly major consideration, everyone would smoke generic cigarettes. Coupons aren't redeemed anywhere near commensurate with their level of availability. The brand's image is the major consideration because it closely addresses the smokers' own real, perceived, or desired image. Consider these examples:

➨ Benson & Hedges—sophisticated

➨ Lucky Strike—no frills, no-nonsense, no filter

➨ Virginia Slims/Eve— feminine

➠ Marlboro—as symbolized by the "Marboro Man" (even when smoked by a woman) independent, a maverick

➠ Newport—an outdoor person, usually identified with the beach, the surf, the woods, symbols of cool streams, outdoor activities

➠ Carleton—reserved, deliberate, conservative

These are seven brands out of hundreds, and each spends millions of dollars to shape and define its image. They spend *millions more* on brand extensions to broaden the image, which we'll look at a bit later.

Few men will be seen smoking Virginia Slims and Eve. The marketers encourage this to be so, just as Lucky Strike was the brand targeted to construction workers over concert pianists.

In surveys of smokers, when asked the question "if your regular brand is not available . . .?" a high frequency answer that they will go somewhere else to buy it rather than accept another brand in its place. The commercial that tried to encourage this some years ago featured the Tareyton cigarette smoker with a black eye and the slogan "I'd rather fight than switch." While indicators are that smokers are not inclined to get physical over the brand issue, they *will* go to another shop to exercise their brand loyalty.

A brand's advertising and its package design are the major factors in determining its image—silver and gold foil, raised embossed lettering, a coat of arms. The choice of the name for a cigarette brand, a name to reflect a certain image, is the clearest example of brand *name* as definition. Consider the names and the images they suggest:

Barclay	Lark
Parliament	Spring

Cambridge	Salem
Benson & Hedges	Newport
Chesterfield	Now
York	Eve
Carleton	Kool
Winston	True
Kent	Malibu

In the left column, the names suggest sophistication, power, elitism, an old English influence. In the right column, the names convey a lighter, more relaxed, less intense, even frivolous mood. As controversial as the issue may be, cigarette smoking by the end of the 1980s was up worldwide, particularly among young women. In the United States, while the number of smokers appears to be declining and television advertising is not permitted, new brands are introduced constantly and—primarily through magazine, newspaper, outdoor advertising, and package—design find image-conscious customers.

Beer.   Beer is another product that many people insist has but one taste, that of beer. Yet, brand loyalty is high, and passions run high. Again, it is the brand *image,* more than the price or ease of availability that helps to define its loyal consumers . . .

Budweiser	Heinekin
Old Style	Dos-Equis
Coors	Corona
Strohs	Amstel
Old Milwaukee	Kirin
Schlitz	

Whether domestic or imported, the choice of beer is as "correct" as the choice of a preferred sports team or a rock band in concert. The choice of beer says more about a consumer's personal perception than the taste of the beer itself. It's the image.

It is widely accepted that word-of-mouth advertising is perhaps the most effective type (and not at this time under any restrictions imposed by the FTC); loyal brand users make excellent endorsers. There is a certain unique pride in the customer commenting—whether about a beer, smoke, sweater, or luggage—"that's my brand."

Ultimately, brand building involves giving the customer what she or he wants with value (price and quality) and in the image the customer is seeking, aspiring to, or at the very least, ready and willing to accept.

Building brand *loyalty* involves *continuing* to serve that customer in a satisfactory way. Again, research is the key. People's tastes change. Know when to change with them and when to remain an anchor in the sea of change.

Is this contradictory?

Sure.

But consider that the typical consumer will change his or her hairstyle (or color), wardrobe, address, and job every so often, yet remain loyal over a lifetime to a certain breakfast cereal or toothpaste. Research will help you define your target audience and track its receptivity to change. Sometimes brand loyalty fades when a consumer feels the product is not maintaining or increasing standards of quality. The consumer feels let down. Sometimes a consumer walks away from a product that's tried to appeal to a newer, wider, younger, or more exclusive market segment . . . and not afforded enough consideration to the "old timers."

Consider the following points:

➡ Know your customer

- ➠ Know what your customer wants

- ➠ Satisfy your customer

- ➠ *Keep* satisfying your customer

- ➠ Know when to stay the same and when to change

- ➠ Use your research

Consumers Will Pay to Advertise Your Product

Premiums encourage brand loyalty. Where once caps, sweatshirts, t-shirts, jackets, or coffee mugs were given away free to promote a brand, consumers today are willing to pay (a lot!) to wear their favorite brand's logo. Let your research tell you if, and to what degree, your customers respond to premiums—offers of dishes, books, towels, records, etc., with or without the brand logo indicated.

Betty Crocker, Campbell Soup, and Duncan Hines are brands that have, over the years, very successfully used cookbooks as both a premium and a separate retail item. The advantage of such a premium is the constant brand reinforcement through the book's presence in the home. Mobil Travel Guides are another example of an item that reinforces the brand's presence without its principal product being represented.

Let your research tell you if your customers use or want coupons for discounts on your (or other related) products. If the answer is yes, offer them. Banks and credit card companies (not your typical companies likely to offer coupons) will often give coupons good for discounts at restaurants or movie theaters. Such offers generate goodwill and repeat business, tangibly saying "thank you" for a customer's loyalty.

Newsletters, magazines, and regular mailings and surveys suggest that a company wants both to give and receive information, enhance value, and keep their name in front of their customers. Philip Morris and Fidelty Investments are only two of several companies publishing slick, colorful magazines that keep their customers informed of a multitude of things, including news of the companies' newest products.

A company's mailing list is not only a very profitable commodity to rent to other companies, it is a great device to *use*. Mail to customers. Include coupons and survey questions that will help you take the pulse of the market and reaffirm your appreciation. At the same time, create and use opportunities to cross-sell your own and perhaps other products.

Credit cards, mileage points, cash back coupons, and trading stamps are a few of the devices developed over the years to build brand loyalty while enhancing value and making things easier for the consumer. They work as well in the 1990s as they did in the 1950s if they are packaged, presented, and promoted in such a way that they are easy to understand, acquire, and access. Many companies offer bonus dollars, point, coupons, etc., for a customer referring another customer into the brand's legions of satisfied customers. Book-of-the-Month Club, Columbia Record Club and others have offered gifts (of course, bearing their name and logo) if a customer brings the brand to the attention of a new customer. It is word-of-mouth advertising paying off—with a payoff.

Catalogs and sale flyers are a way to put something new with your name on it into a consumer's home or business. These items are often kept around (and passed around) for months. Production costs and mailing costs keep going up, and this is an area where many companies feel they cut costs by cutting back. Remember that mailing to customers isn't just an effort to get another order *today;* it is to reinforce your presence in customers' lives. A letter, a catalog cover, a brochure or a postcard that is addressed to an American Express credit card *member,* or a Literary Guild book club *member* or a BMW *driver* or *Newsweek subscriber* reinforces the consumer's relationship to the product or company. Blockbuster Video and West Coast Video don't need to spend so much issuing plastic "membership" cards, when any form of identification (and the rental price) will allow someone to rent tapes. They issue these cards to encourage a sense of "belonging" to a particular group in the hopes that the customer will feel a loyalty to return to that video store instead of renting tapes from the booth at the dry cleaner or grocery store.

Building brand loyalty is taking the steps to make today's customer tomorrow's customer as well.

Review

1. Elements that encourage brand loyalty are:
   a. value (price and quality)
   b. image (personality and reputation)
   c. convenience and ease of availability
   d. satisfaction
   e. service
   f. guarantee or warranty

2. Use continuing research to monitor:
   a. changes in level of customer or market satisfaction
   b. changing public tastes

3. Know your customer and what your customer wants.

4. Develop interactive vehicles such as newsletters and magazines to give and get consumer information.

5. Consider premiums—free or affordable, and accessible—that will make customers feel personally identified with the brand.

6. Consider programs such as those offering points, dollars, discounts, or other benefits for making use of the brand more often.

7. Show gratitude to customers. The bigger the company gets, the more consumers feel distanced from it. In a competitive environment, a clear message of *service* and *appreciation* produces customer loyalty to your product.

8. Use catalogs, sale flyers, credit cards, and membership cards to reinforce the brand's presence in the consumer's life.

9. Be responsive to your customers.

10. Don't promise what you can't deliver. It's the surest way to terminate a customer's loyal relationship with a brand.

Chapter Four

Knowing When the Brand Is in Trouble

"A problem is a chance for you to do your best."

—Duke Ellington

Uh-Oh. What Now?

Ford had a problem with the Pinto's gas tank exploding into flames when struck at even low impact. The fallout from this problem posed a threat not only to Pinto owners, but to the entire Ford Motor Company. Several bottles of Tylenol capsules were laced with poison, and several consumers died after ingesting the tainted product. The company had to worry about surviving. Exxon Oil Company's tanker, the Valdez, left an oil spill off the Alaskan coastline that resulted in the worst environmental disaster in history. These are crises of major proportions—life and death situations. Business must react to situations such as these in ways that address moral, ethical, and legal concerns, delicately balancing them against the fate of the company and its future commercial viability.

But what of the crises of the non-life-threatening variety?

Earlier we noted the name problem of AYDS, the diet plan candy. When your brand name is coincidentally that of a disease that grows to epidemic proportions, it won't help to simply stamp "new and improved" on your package. But I am not trying to jokingly dismiss problems over which a company's fate hangs in the balance. Sometimes brands get into trouble—losing market share or their market altogether—because they were something of a fad product to begin with. Sometimes products are so upstaged by competing products, occasionally even those produced by their own parent company, that they appear to simply give up the fight and die on the vine. Let's consider the wine cooler industry.

For as far back as one can remember ways of mixing drinks, there has been some combination of wine with a carbonated beverage. The champagne cocktail was one, the white wine spritzer another. The 1960s and '70s saw the introduction of Annie Greensprings and Boone's Farm wines. These so-called "pop wines" sold in quart bottles, combined fruit juice flavorings with wine and club soda and seemed the perfect accompaniment to tie-dyed clothing and folk music. As fads and trends were replaced by new fads and trends, and as the brands began to slip, the manufacturers did not reinvent or reposition the product, but treated it as if they were as surprised as everyone else it had done so well in the first place, and let it just fade quietly into the sunset.

In the 1980s virtually the same beverage concept was revived as a "wine cooler," this time in smaller, stylish bottles sold in four- or six-packs, and became, again, a huge success, creating a multimillion dollar beverage category.

And again, as the 1980s passed on, so did most of the '80s tastes and trends . . . including the wine cooler. It was as though society was prepared to simply treat decades as modular units replacing one with the other, style and fads intact. "Trend shops" began appearing as an alternative to the more serious, conservative research organizations. For fees up to a million dollars, firms such as the Brain Reserve, the Trend Union, and Promostyle would advise such clients as Pillsbury, Kodak, and Campbell's Soup on what was— and was likely to be—the next big trend.

Why? What happened to the basics of marketing? Shouldn't the marketing plan have been revised, a new batch of research commissioned and a new ad campaign created to at least salvage, if not breathe new life into the multimillion dollar wine cooler market?

It did appear that some attempt was made to replace, for example, the Bartles & Jaymes characters in the TV ads with a new and more mainstream theme, but perhaps the most curious marketing idea to come out in the 1980s was the idea of giving up on a product or brand as soon as a new one is on the scene.

When a hot new toothpaste with baking soda was successfully launched, so were several more, with manufacturers paying less marketing attention to the solid, established core brands. The baking soda toothpaste, by the way, was from Arm & Hammer, the company that had been suggesting for over 40 years that baking soda be used as toothpaste.

The proliferation of brands continues at high speed. For years, manufacturers concentrated on building brands. If a product's sales flagged, the manufacturer's response might predictably be to add a little something to the product (salt, sugar, bleach, lemon, mint, or whatever) and a little more color to the packaging and roll out the next shipment with "new and improved" emblazoned above the name. A product such as Proctor & Gambles' Tide has been given the new-and-improved treatment so many times over the years, one must wonder if it now bears any resemblance at all to its product ancestor. But it's still selling. *Big*. Proctor & Gamble stayed with the brand, supporting it, improving it, and keeping its visibility high as sudsy new challengers came and went.

How do you know when its time to reposition a product, retire it, or leave it alone?

The market tells you. Sales tell you. Yet, as competition intensifies, reliable research—not *trend data*—can be your best defense against declines in market share. But beyond research, your marketing plan must have action tactics. Just *having* research isn't enough. You need to do something with the information.

Professor Richard Tedlow of the Harvard Graduate School of Business Administration notes, "We have seen how consumer tastes and needs with regard to particular products have changed . . . We have seen how individual firms have changed—how they have sometimes fallen prey to forces that have aged them and robbed them of what made them great."

One reason so many brands stumble is they willingly surrender their USP—their unique selling proposition—choosing to identify themselves with self-serving and generic descriptions.

When Lipper Analytical Services ranks mutual funds in dozens of categories, most of the funds designated as number one in their respective categories rush an ad into the next day's *Wall Street Journal*, each one humbly congratulating itself. So the reader gets to see a dozen or so ads in the same issue of the same paper, headlined "We're number one!"

Putting down the paper, this person may turn on a television set to see a commercial for the number one Ford dealer in town, before the number one Buick dealer's spot comes on. The obvious point is that the consumer is no more impressed by such gratuitous claims than they are by the claims of "fast, dependable service" that are unique to no one anymore and are contradicted by consumer surveys.

In December 1991 Julie Liesse wrote in *Advertising Age,* "Marketers have made it easy for consumers to trade down and tune out presumably venerable brand names by siphoning ad dollars to fund trade promotions . . . by providing all too similar ad messages, by losing the edge in product innovation." She noted that, "As brand loyalty crumbles, marketers look for new answers."

Herb Maneloveg of the New York-based Maneloveg Media Marketing, reacted to the *Ad Age* story, saying, "The true tragedy is that marketers make all kinds of speeches and offer unending press comment, but they do almost nothing to change the way they communicate to their publics who control the destiny of products being marketed. And they seldom come up with quality improvements in their brands to suit consumer needs." Perhaps most damning is his parting shot: "Most advertisers don't seek out answers. They're merely trying to get through their current quarter, forgetting about the brand's future."

Clearly, there is plenty of blame to go around when sales or market share go into a dive. Often, blame is coupled with panic or desperation when careers and big bucks are at stake. And all too often, rather than administrating CPR to a gasping brand, marketers or manufacturers will abandon it for their equivalent answer to "this year's model."

Dave Murphy, president of the Betty Crocker division of General Mills, notes "Brand credibility brings a convenience of decisionmaking to consumers' lives."

With the huge budgets devoted to building this "brand credibility," it is surprising to see companies exhibit such a willingness to pull the plug and treat brands themselves as disposable commodities, choosing to take their chances with a new name and face.

From 1985 to 1991 the number of items carried on the supermarket shelves soared to more than 16,000—an increase of 45.5 percent. With all these new products, one might think the matter of identifying a brand's unique qualities would take on even greater urgency. Alas, the opposite is true. The prevailing wisdom is that, as with a prize fight or the Indy 500, there can only be one winner. One brand, emerging as the category leader, is allowed to dominate while others fire their marketing directors and accept their minor roles, awaiting the next product or variation to reinvigorate their competitive energies.

Occasionally, we see clever exceptions to this number one product dominance strategy. Avis car rentals built its slogan and its most successful advertising campaign around its being the runner-up to the much larger Hertz. Avis' line: "We're # 2. We try harder." The public reacted positively, unaccustomed to hearing anyone admit to not being number one.

Sometimes, however, this can go too far. Some brands appear to think that even making the top ten is satisfactory. Indeed Buick produced a series of ads bragging that it was the only American car to make an independent testing organization's list of top ten cars with fewest complaints or some such thing.

It was number five.

Many marketers believed a curious (and possibly low) point had been reached when a brand would brag about being number five at anything.

The good news for brands is that, with all the brands' faults, consumers still seem to prefer them, largely having gotten over their brief though well-publicized flirtations with generic products. In the 1970s, generic product interest was so great—from creamed corn to bathroom tissue to grapefruit juice to beer and cigarettes—that store aisle after aisle was a long row of white and black packages, flaunting its deliberate absence of personality. By the 1980s, generic product sales had plummeted. People wanted to know what they were buying and took considerable interest in the credibility and reputations of those who offered it to them.

The bad news for brands is that "private label" products, which had never been taken all that seriously in the competitive sense, are doing much better. Dunkin' Donuts sells its own brand of coffee (whole bean or ground) for patrons to take home by the pound. Over the years it has built a fiercely loyal and devoted clientele. Eight O'Clock Coffee, a brand originally introduced by the old A&P grocery chain, is on a par with gourmet quality brands in some quarters. Not only major chain stores, but Ma and Pa grocery, restaurant, and specialty stores are doing well with their own signatures—private labels—on jams, jellies, salad dressings, candies, and even clothing that not that long ago would have been a much less respected alternative to a major brand.

Richard Furash, national director of consumer products for the accounting firm of Deloitte & Touche's consultancy group notes, "The problem with branding . . . is that consumer goods marketers are not investing in their brands . . . (and as consumers look for ways to save money) they're finding the quality of the private label products are better."

Many observers add that a reason brands get into trouble is they operate in such a vacuum, perhaps viewing themselves alone or only against a major competitor, forgetting the perspective of the consumer. While major brands are beating their chests and bragging, what's the value to customers?

For years, a major complaint, often repeated and widely publicized, is about the clutter, the overwhelming number of advertisements and commercials to which a consumer is subjected on an ongoing basis. Advertisers and their ad agencies speak freely about it, acknowledge it is a concern, and then go about their business, the result being apparent indifference to the consumer's plight. As difficult as the clutter problem is to solve, it really needs to be addressed more seriously; the object of the advertising is, after all, to be noticed and remembered. Consider that if a two-minute TV commercial break carries—between the commercials themselves, local and network promos, billboards, and station identifications—somewhere around ten to twelve identifiable messages and announcements, consumer recall would likely be around two or three.

On the print side, in Sunday newspapers and the most popular monthly magazines, the situation is not much better, except that the shelf life of the ads favors print. This is not very good news to the healthiest brand, much less to the one in trouble and in need of the greatest impact it can create. Despite the recognition and professed concern, the reason clutter continues to grow, of course, is the high cost of doing business, which can only be offset by cramming as much advertising as possible into the allotted spaces.

One should not, as fashionable as the practice is these days, single out the media for blame. Advertisers themselves take too many shortcuts. *Advertising Age* makes the point that, "Despite the care that manufacturers expend on packaging, their products are often merchandised in haphazard fashion."

Notes Sid Doolittle of McMillan/Doolittle, a retail consulting firm, "The marketing world has underestimated some of the changes that have taken place at the retail level. The marketplace will never be the same again."

Adds Christopher Hunt of Willard Bishop Consulting, "There are floor displays all over the place . . . It's a style that in general runs contrary to the careful merchandising philosophy . . ."

Whoever told marketers that cluttered display areas entice customers, much less show the product in its best light?

Shelves are there for a reason, and so are the aisles, display cases, and counters. Clutter is a consumer turn off, whether in the aisles of Macy's or on prime-time Sunday night television.

Create displays that fit the space. They will be noticed better and show the product better. Of course, economics suggests that you put the most product in the space. But it's a mistake to crowd a display area and highly self-defeating. Two solutions to broadcast and cable clutter—as well as print clutter—are:

1. Consider clearly segregating advertising from programming and editorial material. In print, insert catalogs in newspapers and mailings, or set up free-standing displays. Catalogs, when well done, get read and passed along for a far longer time than the usual magazine. The framework allows creative people wider parameters as well.

    In broadcasting, a clearly separated, say, eight-minute, segment at the end of the program might resemble a mini home shopping program that offered video (or audio) versions of "blue light specials"—discounts, contests, or special incentives to attentive shoppers. This process poses a tremendous challenge to ad agencies to create commercials that are entertaining enough to hold an audience, which is what they are supposed to do. Entertain and inform, don't punish an audience.

2. Simply, be more creative. Much of television and radio's answer to standing out in clutter is to be louder. Advertising that is funny, uses music effectively, is well written and well photographed, and, in short, gives the consumer reason to pay attention, gets noticed. Noise and lack of creativity, clarity, and information make people resent advertising and label it as insulting and intrusive.

A decline in interest in the brand is not always simply the result of bad ads poorly placed or of the crowded, clumsy use of retail space. It is all too often the result of a manufacturer or marketer moving away from the factors that determined why people believed they needed or wanted the brand in the first place. While not every situation is the same, a basic outline can be constructed to help rebuild or reposition a sagging brand.

When is it too late?

The market will tell you. Sometimes public tastes change so radically, the situation analysis seems to write itself:

➡ Fuel efficiency's in, big cars are out.

➡ Health consciousness-raising says it's tough times ahead for foods with high fat, sodium, and cholesterol.

➡ A recessionary economy means a smaller market for big-ticket items.

➡ An increase in environmental awareness suggests a decrease in interest in products that are polluting or non-recyclable.

➡ A major product or company scandal makes starting over a more realistic alternative to riding it out.

But if, as has been suggested, the brand's declining pattern is for reasons other than the preceding five examples, consider how we might create a basic map for the return to stability and growth:

➠ Analyze how in its early days the brand broke from the pack or met a need that had gone unnoticed. What's changed?

➠ Revise your marketing plan if you need to. A good marketing plan isn't chiseled in stone; it's flexible enough to accommodate changes in the market climate.

➠ Don't operate in a vacuum. Let your research tell you how people's attitudes may have changed toward your company or product, alone and relative to the competition. Are you considered environmentally unfriendly? Overpriced? Old fashioned? Too representative of an era gone by?

➠ Keep your visibility high. One of the most common and most absurd decisions businesses continue to make is to cut advertising, public relations, and promotions budgets when times get tough and sales drop. This is when you need visibility the most; it's the time when your ads are your greatest *investment* in your brand's future.

➠ Take nothing for granted. Don't assume that because your brand has been around for a long time that your target market knows you and all you have to offer. Re-evaluate your price/quality/image, and if the story is worth telling, tell it. If it's not worth telling, then your value must be redefined and publicized.

➡ Remember the USP—the unique selling proposition—the reason people should want what you have to sell.

➡ Some of the best names in the business faltered before catching on big (Jell-O, Kleenex, 7-Up, Timex, and Pepsi are a few), while others (Chrysler comes to mind) *came back* big after being virtually counted out. A positive attitude, the desire to succeed, a good marketing plan, and a strong financial commitment to support the plan can keep a quality brand alive in rough or changing times.

Review

1. Conduct and use research. Don't wait for the bottom to drop. Track sales trends (your own and your competitors) and market trends and act on needs to reposition your brand.

2. Don't give up on a product prematurely. Very often the media announces "the next big trend" and the public doesn't bite.

3. Don't assume as you become more successful that your customers care about your success. Stay focused on providing benefits. Being number one is good news for your bank, but your customers always should be reminded of what you've got for *them*.

4. Improve what needs to be improved—product, price, distribution, packaging, advertising, public relations. It's easier the earlier you begin to see the

need. Waiting isn't (always) fatal, but it's more expensive.

5. The best way to beat the clutter is to be *good*. Make your brand advertising stand out from the other advertising the way you make your product stand out from your competition. Be creative and create ads loaded with reasons to take notice.

6. Be sensitive and responsive to changes in the marketplace and in public tastes and perceptions.

7. Keep your marketing plan flexible and don't operate in a vacuum.

8. Stay visible. You're not really *saving* if you cut advertising and public relations at a time you need visibility and goodwill the most.

9. Keep your unique selling proposition in front of your customer.

10. React honestly to change.

Section II

GOING BEYOND BRANDING

*How Brands Create a Niche and Remain
Competitive and Responsive to
Public Demand*

Chapter Five

Brand Extension

The Art or Science of Starting a Family . . . of Products

Stepping Out

Professor David A. Aaker describes the practice of managing brand equity as capitalizing on the value of the name, and it is certainly that. Such capitalizing can go in several directions. The purest and simplest way is to work with the core product of the brand, nurturing, publicizing, advertising, and enhancing its position. As it becomes more and better established, more highly regarded as a brand of choice, price increases are more easily accepted by the marketplace. Distribution and shelf space, store position, or listing order are more easily enhanced. Word-of-mouth references raise its level of familiarity. The establishment of real value in the brand name is an achievement of significant proportions.

Yet, what has made brand equity such a hot topic among marketers is not merely its achievement, but its extension in two major directions. One is the area of *licensing,* allowing the brand name and the trademark to be used by someone else, often in categories and industries far removed from that of the brand itself. The second area is that of *line* or *brand extension* in the form of new product offshoots of the original brand.

In the first area, licensing, about which volumes could be written, the importance to the brand is on several levels. Licensing generates tremendous revenue when done successfully. The Disney Studios, for example, licenses its name, image, and its catalog of characters to hundreds of manufacturers worldwide for reproduction on shirts, shoes, sleepwear, bedding, toys, books, records, jewelry, furniture, school supplies, foods, and much more. Disney Stores carrying nothing but their own labeled merchandise are proving highly successful in malls around the world. A catalog of Disney merchandise broadens avenues of availability. Disney's business, of course, is making movies and operating a cable television channel and several theme parks and hotels, but the revenue gained from these prime ventures is enhanced or surpassed by that generated by putting their name on products in which they have little or no manufacturing role—or capital investment.

McDonald's, Coca-Cola, and Playboy are three of many major corporations that have licensed their names and logos to lines of clothing. After some initial interest, curiosity, or fad/cult treatment, the McDonald's and Coca-Cola fashions faded. Playboy continued for many years, however, to sell its name to some very pricey items that tried to carry the image of the Playboy, as defined in its magazine, into real life.

Licensing can be as diverse and sprawling as including the franchises and, in effect, leasing a company's technologies or systems to others. This type of licensing is increasingly popular as brands seek to expand into other countries, utilizing the brand's own proprietary name and processes by local companies more conversant with the climate of the regulatory and public environment. It can significantly preserve the brand company's own capital as well.

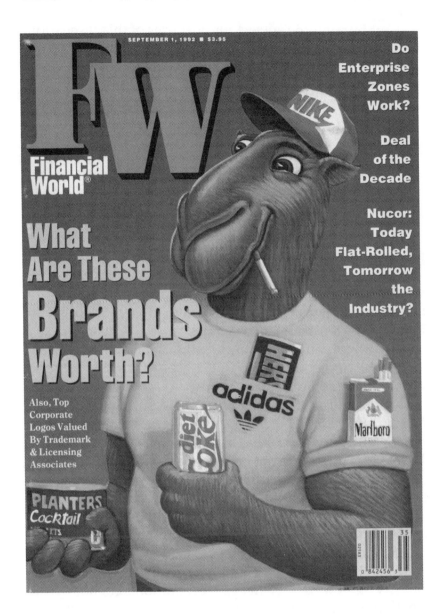

There's nothing very subtle about the importance business attaches to brand equity—or its dollar value—as noted in the seven major brands pictured on this *Financial World* magazine cover. (Courtesy of *Financial World*. Used with permission.)

But limiting the subject for purposes of this discussion, the licensing of a name and trademark affords a brand numerous benefits including the following:

1.   Revenue generation.

2.   Greater brand name visibility.

3.   The ability to utilize the advertising and marketing apparatus (and budget) of others to advance the brand.

The downside of this, of course, is that when the licensed product fails to do well, the brand's good name, in which much has been invested, could be tarnished or otherwise devalued.

Licensing has evolved as an enormous profit center for the entertainment industry. Although always used profitably to a degree (as when cowboy stars like Roy Rogers and Gene Autrey could be found smiling at fans from lunch boxes, coloring books, toys, and clothes) it reached art form status when entertainment industry marketers sold merchandise rights for dozens of items of such properties as *Batman, Star Wars, Peter Pan,* and *Dick Tracy,* generating millions of dollars more in revenue than the films themselves. This point was not lost on corporate America, which now boasts merchandise catalogs of logo-imprinted goods from ashtrays to cuff links to neckties and much more.

Consumers can buy banks, cups, and pens in the shape of Planters' "Mr. Peanut," or beach toys shaped and colored to resemble Life Savers candy or Charlie, the Star-Kist tuna, or comic books featuring Kellogg's Tony the Tiger. Items such as these were giveaways a generation ago, but by the 1980s, they were significant revenue generators, both fashionable and collectible. Nostalgia memorabilia worth big money, centered around Mickey Mouse or Shirley Temple items, now added Ovaltine shaker mugs, cereal bowls with

Kellogg's Snap, Crackle, and Pop figures or the Campbell's Soup kids on them. Soda fountain glasses bearing the Coca-Cola logo are a perennial hit.

Of course, the big revenue is not from waiting for nostalgia to create a desire for your logo on merchandising, but from hanging it on items the market wants now, as Nike and Reebok have proved, for example, by putting their names on products unrelated to their own sportswear.

The second major area in which brands are stepping out is line extensions. Here too, though, there are sub-categories and differing definitions. That is, once a product was introduced, some thought it was being extended when it was later offered in small, medium, and large sizes. Then came the giant economy size and its opposite extreme the "mini," individual, or personal size. A food brand speaks proudly of having some 270 SKUs (stock keeping units). To the uninitiated, this may appear to be 270 separate products; But it is actually about 75 different food products (or fewer), many of which are offered in several different sizes. So, does one product in five or six sizes constitute a line extension? To some, yes; to others, no.

What about shapes? Most major pasta companies offer basically the same pasta in the form of spaghetti, shells, lasagna noodles and anything from "elbows" to "bow-tie" pasta. So if six or eight shape variations are offered, does it constitute a brand's line extension? The answer is the same: yes, to some and not really to others.

The same question arises in the flavors area. The old definition would have been that a product (ice cream or soft drinks, for example) offered in orange, cherry, and lemon flavor was simply one product available in three flavors. Add strawberry and to some, you now have one product in four flavors; to others you have four products. And, depending on who owns the companies, they can both be right. The ice cream company that boasts 31 flavors doesn't really think it has launched a brand extension or changed the product line when it adds number 32. Yet, the soft drink company that introduces a new diet or caffeine-free beverage most definitely considers this introduction not just an addition, but a *major* extension of the brand.

John Loden, president of the marketing communications firm Vicom/FCB, suggests "In today's fragmented market no single product can appeal to a wide enough group of consumers to maintain a brand-based franchise. In order to attract and hold sophisticated consumers, a brand must offer a variety of choices within its line."

But Mr. Loden also warns of the process of cannibalization, the extended brand product drawing away from the core brand itself, rather than the competition. This has always represented a dilemma of sorts to marketers in every industry. If you *don't* offer the new product, you risk losing a customer who may believe your competition is being more responsive to the current needs of the marketplace. If you *do* offer the product, you risk taking the customer away from your own core or parent product brand. Obviously, the latter choice is the preferred alternative, albeit an expensive one.

Some marketers suggest stabilizing the core brand at the maximum strength before attempting to brand extend. Often, however, the market won't wait. When the 1980s market trend ran to light, low fat, cholesterol free, caffeine free, all natural and recyclable, many brand equity-building plans were interrupted and had to be revised to reflect the shift in the marketplace. Sometimes a brand repositions, sometimes it becomes more than a single brand.

The debate on brand extension runs from those who believe marketers should define and stick with building and selling the benefits of a good product and not to fall victim to whims of a fickle public, to those who believe that to sell product, one must give the public what it wants.

John Loden offers that "in today's competitive environment where rapid line extension is the key to growth, new products must be introduced quickly and frequently. To ensure the acceptance of these new products by consumers, brand positionings must be expanded through a conscious, systematic process." This sounds like a well-developed marketing plan with a more long-range view than merely what the public wants *today*.

Yet, in a highly detailed examination of the subject of brand marketing, *Financial World* writer Alexandra Ourusoff notes that, "in a saturated marketplace, new product introductions and brand extensions are not the answer they once were ... More than 80 percent of the products introduced (in 1991) were brand extensions. Experience suggests that 87 percent of those products are likely to fail."

Al Ries and Jack Trout profess that "logic is on the side of brand extension. Truth, unfortunately, is not."

Their conclusion is based on examinations of some of the best names in the business attempting to transfer the power, recognition, and high approval ratings of their brands to the new products, with results ranging from unsuccessful to embarrassing in some cases. Among their examples: popular Dial soap's poor showing with Dial shampoo and top-selling Bayer aspirin's most unfortunate introduction of an aspirin-free product. Bayer had spent years and millions establishing its reputation as *the* choice in aspirin pain reliever, only to see its market share drop as Tylenol pain reliever won the match. Undaunted, Bayer keeps repackaging, renaming, and repitching its alternative product and charging up the hill again.

A Quick Glance at the Shelf in the Pharmacy

Not very long ago, six products were common household pain relievers and cold remedies: Bayer aspirin, Bufferin,

Anacin, Excedrin, Dristan, and Tylenol. Each was launched and promoted as a single product. By 1992 these six products were represented by some 43 products, and more can be expected as tablets, caplets, and geltabs multiply.

Anacin
Maximum Strength Anacin
Aspirin Free Anacin
Maximum Strength Aspirin
    Free Anacin
Aspirin Free Anacin PM

Bayer Aspirin
Bayer Select
Bayer Select Sinus Pain
    Reliever
Maximum Strength Bayer
    Select
Extra Strength Bayer Plus
Bayer Children's Aspirin

Bufferin
Bufferin AF Nite Time
Bufferin Caplets
Bufferin Extra Strength
Bufferin Arthritis Strength

Dristan
Dristan Nasal Spray

Dristan 12-hour Nasal
    Spray
Dristan Cold
Dristan Cold Maximum
    Strength
Dristan Cold and Flu
Dristan Allergy
Dristan Sinus

Excedrin
Sinus Excedrin
Aspirin Free Excedrin
Aspirin Free Excedrin PM
Aspirin Free Excedrin IB
Aspirin Free Excedrin Dual
    (for headaches and upset
    stomach)

Tylenol
Tylenol Cold
Tylenol Cold
    No Drowsiness Formula
Extra Strength Tylenol PM
Tylenol Liquid Pain
    Reliever

Tylenol Sinus	Junior Strength Tylenol
Children's Tylenol	Infant Tylenol Drops
Children's Tylenol Drops	Infant Tylenol Elixir
Children's Tylenol Elixir	Infant Tylenol Suspension
Children's Tylenol Suspension Liquid	Liquid

Most of these products are offered in a variety of package quantity sizes and various forms, such as tablets, caplets, liquid, and gelcaps (most capsules are being abandoned following cases of product tampering). Are these choices so plentiful because the public demands such a range, or are the brands more likely trying to outdo one another?

Some evidence points to the latter.

Indeed, the choices of extra strength, maximum strength, IB, AF, and PM serve to confuse the public who simply want pain relief, not to judge the pain reliever olympics.

Further, shelf space is at a premium. For a well-stocked shelf to accommodate a brand extension in its various sizes and forms, it must be at the expense of another product. Of course, this could be another case of survival of the fittest, with the weaker brands relegated to the back room, but a good marketer needs to be sensitive to problems that confront the retailer and the consumer. Of course, a top selling brand will carry some clout, but retailers often resent having to carry a brand extension that has not earned a clear right to command shelf space.

Make certain your research supports your decision to extend the brand and *share the research* with both the retailer and the consumer. Telling people why they should care about what you've done and, in fact, that it responds to an identified need or desire is, again, good marketing. Four variations of six products, each in three sizes, forces choices some people may not appreciate having to make. The process of developing, producing, distributing, and promoting is also very expensive. Remember old rules like "less is more," and determine whether your resources might not be better committed to producing fewer variations and focusing more on building and maintaining the brand.

This would seem to make a case for deciding *against* brand extension.

Not at all.

It *is*, however, a strong suggestion to aim at the target by first lining it up in your sight. If the opinions of experts are anything to go by, the hot and heavy tendency toward brand extension is more an exercise in competitive one-upmanship than it is a response to the marketplace.

Al Ries and Jack Trout compare the brand name to a rubber band, noting "it will stretch, but not beyond a certain point. Furthermore, the more you stretch a name the weaker it becomes."

Consider how the simple process of ordering a cup of coffee in a restaurant used to be followed by a response of "thank you." Now the usual response is "regular or decaf?"

How long might it be before ordering a Coke is followed by the question "Is that regular Coke Classic, Coke II, diet, caffeine free, cherry, diet cherry, clear, or diet clear?"

Campbell's

Consider a position such as that of David Aaker, that the brand extension decision is in effect a strategic one since the extensions build upon the associations of the core brand. He cites as an example the Campbell Soup Company, which, already dominant in the prepared soups category (with a 75 percent market share in 1992), launched Manhandler,

Homestyle, and Special Request, in addition to distinct lines of Chunky Home Cookin', Golden Classic, Gold Label, Creamy Natural, Soup Du Jour, Cookbook Classics, and French Chef.

"Each of these," Professor Aaker notes "was costly to establish and added to potential for confusion. Eventually, the cost in dollars and confusion to establish such a variety of names may surpass their value in terms of offering associations."

Indeed.

To go a step further, there is not only a dubious value to the parent brand in extensions such as these, but virtually a store section full of product that appears to be *competing* with the Campbell brand and possibly devaluing the name. Does it make more sense in a case such as this for Campbell's to simply continue, as it had for years, adding to its ever-growing variety of flavors, increasing its category dominance?

Clearly, consumers would agree to sample, enjoy, and repurchase the offshoots, but at what expense? If it is at the expense of the original Campbell's Soup, it is brand cannibalization, not extension.

It is uniquely challenging in such situations to respond to trends: the marketplace is ripe and a whole new generation is ready for premium quality, premium price, all natural, etc. So you introduce your "gold label" premium price/quality extension. But you've been telling your loyal customers for years that you use only the finest quality ingredients and that such quality needn't cost more. What to do?

One choice is the "remember how much you loved it?" approach in which the familiar name is out in a new surrounding where it is appreciated by a whole new generation that understands quality and why the good things last.

Choice two is in the direction of a clearly *segmented* market over a *fragmented* market. Rather than diluting the brand itself with a spin-off "subbrand," let your research guide you through the familiar steps again, only this time to be applied to a *segment* of the market, not the whole market. For example, your product appeals to everyone, but a baby boomer demographic group wants to visibly create a personality for itself different from both the previous generation and the mainstream consumer in particular. They want to feel . . . special. Remember that the basic points of a marketing plan apply to extensions and spin-off products:

➠ Situational Analysis

➠ Objectives

➠ Strategy

➠ Tactic

➠ Budget

Only this time we're narrowing our sights. An early guess is that a brand extension won't be the answer. More likely the answer will have its own name (clearly distancing itself from its parentage), and the name will probably include a word like "special," "premium," or "choice."

Ernest and Julio Gallo, proud as it was of its successful line of moderately priced table wines, knew to keep its name well out of sight in launching the successful Bartles & Jaymes wine coolers. The target market for the product would likely not have been receptive to the product had it been associated with Gallo.

Wrong image.

It needed its own identity for its own segment.

What's in a Name?

WHAT THE WORLD'S TOP BRANDS ARE WORTH.

BY ALEXANDRA OURUSOFF
WITH MICHAEL OZANIAN, PAUL B. BROWN AND JASON STARR
Research Assistants: Isabelle Groc and Meenakshi Panchapakesan

NEW CONSUMER PRODUCTS CAME FLOOD-ing on to the market during the Eighties in unprecedented numbers. Ten years ago, the average supermarket carried somewhere between 12,000 and 15,000 items, according to A&P Vice President Michael Rourke. Today that number has swollen to 45,000.

Only now are we beginning to realize the full impact of that tidal wave. The cost of introducing a new consumer product has risen to as much as $100 million. But the odds of success remain no greater than one in 10.

While the value of the well-known brands that will be guaranteed facings

on the shelf has soared as a result, main-taining those brand names against this onslaught has become more challenging.

To adjust to this harsher reality, con-sumer product companies are refocus-ing their attention on supporting their best-sellers and divesting themselves of everything else. Pfizer recently sold its Coty cosmetics subsidiary. Gerber has put its Buster Brown apparel division on the block. Ralston Purina has announced plans to spin off Continental Baking, maker of Wonder bread and Hostess Twinkies, and Coors continues to shop all but its beer division.

Here, for example, is how William D.

Smithburg, chairman and CEO of Quaker Oats, explained the divestiture trend to shareholders in his latest annual report: "With the successful spin-off of Fisher-Price, Quaker is now focused solely on grocery products for the first time in over 20 years. How will the com-pany create shareholder value with this all-grocery portfolio? To drive value for shareholders, you need strong brands, because brands with leading market share positions generate above-average profitability and cash flow. Our portfolio has that brand strength."

And what is Quaker's portfolio of con-sumer brands worth today? Good ques-

tion. As with other consumer products companies, Quaker's brands are by far its most valuable assets. Yet under generally accepted accounting principles (GAAP), those assets do not appear on the balance sheet except as a nominal amount. Even Quaker management would have a hard time quantifying those values because a standard valuation technique simply does not exist.

Yet there is clearly a growing need for more precise ways of monitoring changes in brand value in this crowded marketplace, if only to improve response time to market challenges. So FW assigned a team of six writers the task of constructing a brand valuation methodology that could in time become the standard.

Here's what they came up with:

The most rigorous technique currently available for product brand valuation, in our opinion, is that used by the Interbrand Group, an international brand consulting firm in the U.K. Borrowing from Interbrand's methodology, after calculating total brand sales, we subtract cost of goods sold, selling, general and administrative expenses and depreciation to derive operating profits. But since the objective is to determine the value of the brand name, an amount equal to what could be earned on the basic, or generic, version of the product had to be deducted. To this "adjusted" operating income figure a tax rate is applied to get net brand profits. Finally, a multiple is applied to determine the value of the brand. For a further explanation, see page 46.

Using Interbrand's method, FW estimated corporate numbers based on interviews with competitors, consultants and industry experts. For corporate logos, FW used Trademark & Licensing Associates, Inc., based in La Jolla, Cal. The premise of their method is that the best measure of a logo's value is what

Budweiser.

CHANEL

a third party will pay to rent it, based on licensing and royalty agreements.

We began with a list of the world's strongest brands, as determined by Interbrand. Next, we separated these into product brands, such as Camel cigarettes, and corporate brands, such as Johnson & Johnson. The values of 15 corporate brands and 42 product brands that appear on pages 47 and 48, respectively, are for the brands who figures seemed most reliable.

Looking over the first list, it's clear that Hennessy, Louis Vuitton, Coke, Tampax and Barbie are worth over twice what they generate in annual sales because their worldwide recognition and established marketing support generates both high market share and above-average operating margins.

Operating margins vary significantly even in the same industry, however. Take Del Monte and Green Giant, for example. Why is the Del Monte brand worth $1.6 billion, or 71% of sales, while Green Giant is valued at $443 million, or 44% of sales? Largely because the Del Monte brand, which is owned by four companies, generates a combined operating margin of 10%, compared with only 7% for Green Giant, which is owned by the U.K.'s Grand Metropolitan.

Brand names such as Coke, Kleenex and Xerox not only become "household words," they become generic in the minds of many, representing the product as well as its competitors. (From *Financial World*. Used with permission.)

Mainstream versus Niche Marketing

Segmentation, fragmentation, niche—there are more ways today than ever before to remind marketers that sometimes the best strategy is not to be right for everyone and that one size needn't always fit all.

The general public, a specific market segment, or a specialty niche may all be answers to the question "What's my target market?"

Johnson Wax's popular furniture polish, Pledge, was a leading brand in regular or lemon-scented aerosol spray. Environmental concerns spurred non-aerosol pump-spray bottles.

Johnson Wax extended its long top-selling Pledge furniture polish to include lemon-scented and "spring fresh" versions. Later additions included Wood Rich moisturizer, Pledge Household Cleaner and pump-spray and saturated disposable sheet versions of popular aerosol products.

Crest toothpaste is for everyone, young and old, regardless of language or income. At least it *can* be. The product in its original form meets the needs of virtually everyone. But maybe a part of your market prefers a gel formula, believing it represents an important improvement on the old paste. Or perhaps they want a stand-up pump dispenser, which is a bit more modern in its packaging design than the time-worn tube. Or maybe you believe that a cutout at the end of the tube which dispenses the toothpaste in a star shape would appeal to a children's formula.

When you can identify a segment of the market that has unique characteristics or its own responses not fully in agreement with the mainstream, you are addressing a *niche market*: younger, seniors, regional tastes, age/generation-specific, ethnic, different levels of affluence.

If the product is a good one and is doing the job, why create a niche extension, thus diluting or cannibalizing the brand and the budget?

Answer one is that maybe (hopefully) you've learned from your research and sales data that the product has a greater appeal in a specific area. Concentrating on that niche may or may not warrant an extension. We may be looking at a repositioning of the product to that niche.

Answer two is that (again, hopefully) you have allowed enough flexibility in your marketing plan to accommodate things you learn as you go and which may create an opening for an extension or other type of change. For example, a terrific shampoo does all that it promises—hair is clean and manageable, etc.—but, alas, leaves a "brassy" look on white or gray hair. The answer to this is to offer a brand extension specifically for this segment of the market. Another answer is to determine how large a segment that group represents and, perhaps deciding it is not a potentially large enough group to accommodate, simply adding a warning to the product's label and conceding that, while you've got a swell product, it's not for everyone. The marketing imagination can help you come up with ideas for a myriad of products, but is your objective to actually *have* a myriad of products or is it to have products people need and want and that you can afford to create, produce, and sell at a profit?

Maclean's

Maclean's toothpaste was neither a successful core product nor a successful extension. It was, however, noteworthy enough at the time to inspire at least several imitators from major companies who feared it *might* succeed at their expense, costing them market share and creating a need for niche reaction products. Maclean's was introduced as an "adult" toothpaste, the first brand of toothpaste in memory to not even hint at its pleasant taste.

There wasn't one. Its message was of a "powerful whitening ingredient" and while it tested well for strength, its medicine-like taste kept consumers from coming back for more. The product was reformulated to add a dash of peppermint, but by then the marketplace had already made up its mind, and Maclean's toothpaste joined the list of rare, hard-to-find brands. The brand might have done better had it simply lowered its sights and accepted a position as a niche brand and been content with a smaller market share.

Ultra Brite

Ultra Brite toothpaste saw potential in Maclean's promise of an "adult brand for extra whiteness" and quickly rushed out a similar product with a similarly unpleasant taste. The difference was that *its* quick peppermint reformulation was launched with a huge ad campaign, all but abandoning the whiteness hook and promising "Ultra Brite gives your mouth sex appeal." This slogan was a hit. Marketers know that not all campaigns built around themes promising sex appeal sell products, but they do tend to get attention and that attention gave Ultra Brite the time it needed to help develop its niche. Ultra Brite is a product of the Colgate-Palmolive Company, which chose to launch it as a product with an identity of its own, rather than a risk a failure of something called perhaps "Colgate Ultra Brite" which, had it failed, conceivably would have damaged the brand equity of the hugely successful and dominant core product.

Colgate and Crest

Colgate toothpaste is Colgate-Palmolive Company's flagship product and a solid success for generations. Crest toothpaste is the best selling dental care name from the brand giant Proctor & Gamble. These two category heavyweights aimed for neither niche marketing nor sex appeal, but instead have, over the years, exercised their considerable muscle through successive brand extensions aimed at protecting their market share: fluoride, gels, tartar-control formulas, stars, sparkles, kids' formulas, and baking soda versions in standard tubes, pumps, stand-up tubes, and dispensers. At literally the first hint of a serious competitive threat, these two brands rolled out the extra-ingredient or "new and improved" extension. This type of market-wide response is normally only achievable if:

1. Research data is so current and so accurate as to definitively reflect the pulse of the marketplace and

2. If a company has massive resources to produce, package, distribute, and publicize the new product extension—and do it with great speed.

This would certainly suggest why and how the biggest brands remain the biggest brands. It is in large part due to having the physical and financial resources to react quickly and give the public what it wants. Colgate and Crest have not strayed far afield, limiting their non-toothpaste extensions to toothbrushes and dental floss.

But obviously, even giants misstep from time to time.

Pall Mall

In the cigarettes category, for example, in the 1960s Pall Mall was a major brand. In fact, it was the *number one* cigarette brand in 1964 with a market share of more than 14 percent. By 1986, however, it had earned great-brand-of-the-past status with a market share of less than 3 percent, despite its aggressive attempt to chase the changing tastes of smokers by introducing Pall Mall filters, Pall Mall Golds, Pall Mall 100s, and Pall Mall Menthol 100s. One possible reason for the brand's decline and fall might have been its clumsy shift in the pronunciation of its name. Insignificant as it may seem, this can have major image ramifications. In radio and TV ads for years, despite its spelling, the brand was pronounced pell-mell. Abruptly, coinciding with the introduction of the brand extensions, the company began saying it (was pronounced) pawl-mawl. As an expression "pell-mell" means to mix things up; as a proper name, it was a London street historically catering to men. In either case, the American cigarette had confused and, ultimately, lost its identity. As a brand it had lacked a focused image, something key to cigarette marketing in particular.

In as late as the 1950s, cigarettes could be mainstream (male and female, white collar and blue collar), but by the 1960s images were being defined: rugged, mild, upscale, no-nonsense. A brand that had survived and prospered in

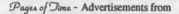

The Philip Morris Company kept its finger on the pulse of the marketplace and put its resources behind building such brand successes as Marlboro and Virginia Slims, while allowing other brands to fade away including Multifilter, Paxton and its once powerful namesake brand. (Philip Morris ad courtesy of *Pages of Time*, Goodlettsville, TN. Used with permission.)

the mainstream at a time when that was possible seemed to lack the personality or clear strength to hold its base as taste and images changed. Pall Mall, at the end of its popularity, lacked a unique selling proposition. When its customer asked why it should be the brand of choice, it didn't have a persuasive response. It was neither for one nor for all.

Virginia Slims

In marked contrast, is the cigarette category's major niche success of recent times, Virginia Slims, which the creators wisely chose not to call Philip Morris Fems or some such patronizing name. Taking notice of the increasing acceptance and popularity (not to mention publicity) surrounding the women's movement, the Philip Morris Company introduced in 1968 with a massive advertising campaign aimed at independent, liberated women—or those who wanted to cast themselves in that image. The campaign's slogan "You've come a long way, baby" has become a classic in modern advertising (although usually forgotten is the somewhat less strong second line "You've got your own cigarette!") By the 1990s such copy would probably never see daylight, dismissed as patronizing, but the brand and its largely unaltered message has survived more than 25 years.

Philip Morris could have repositioned its own sagging namesake brand in ads with only women models and appropriate feminist-oriented copy points, or it could have extended one of its other brands. The bold introduction of a brand that knew what it wanted to be, that told men, still the statistically larger percentage of smokers, "this one's not for you," was a calculated exercise in niche marketing that paid off. Except for the simultaneous introduction of a menthol companion brand, there have been no attempts to extend the brand. The niche proved a profitable place to be.

Leaders of the Pack

Marlboro

One-time leading brand Pall Mall floundered because it failed to define its personality and solidify its place. Virginia Slims succeeded because it found its niche and exploited it effectively. Current category leader Marlboro earned its number one status by finding a strategy and a positioning statement that worked and staying with it for decades.

The European president of Marlboro, Aleardo Buzzi, summed up the company's position saying, "We are the number one brand in the world. What we wanted was to promote a particular image of adventure, of course, of virility . . . "

He certainly can say they did that. Marlboro is not only the biggest selling cigarette in the world, it is the *world's largest selling packaged goods product*. A product of the Philip Morris Company, as a brand Marlboro is valued at $31 billion, according to industry analysts. Of the approximately 400 brands of cigarettes in 1992, Marlboro was number one, with a 20.9 percent market share, almost a half a percentage point gain from the prior year and more than double that of its closest rival, Winston (which posted 8.2 percent market share).

Marlboro is an amazing success story both as a leading brand and as a classic of modern advertising. In 1992 you could have asked anyone what came to mind when they heard the word "Marlboro" and the likely response would have been "The Marlboro Man"—the rugged cowboy from the cigarette ad, established in the TV commercials. But cigarette TV commercials vanished from U.S. screens in 1971. Since then the brand has been represented in print and outdoor ads in the U.S. and in numerous promotional mailings. Yet the image and the bold, rolling, western musical theme remains still vivid more than 20 years later. The Marlboro Man remains one of the most successful advertising campaigns of all time. The brand, now promoted in some 180 countries, had a 1992 ad budget of $118 million ... and, again, that's with no U.S. TV or radio.

"The Marlboro man is almost a cliché of the power of marketing," notes journalist Eric Clark, adding that "Marlboro advertising is perhaps the most blatantly escapist of all cigarette advertising. It offers transformation for the harried, rushed, and crowded urban man to the open spaces, freshness, and the elemental toughness and simplicity of Marlboro country."

Using the expanded campaign line "Come to where the flavor is. Come to Marlboro country," the brand embarked upon an extension of its own. (See Figure 5.1.) From the original, rugged, masculine image wrapped in a classic red

Figure 5.1 **The Marlboro Family Tree (Almost)—A vertical line where everyone lived happily together.**

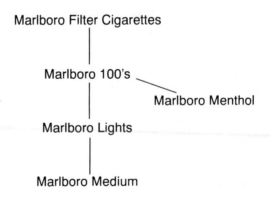

Marlboro Filter Cigarettes

Marlboro 100's

Marlboro Menthol

Marlboro Lights

Marlboro Medium

Available in pack or box (a total of 10 different ways) the world's best-selling cigarette is also the world's largest-selling package goods product: more than $3 billion in sales in 1992.

and white pack, the brand reached for a touch of class when the red was replaced by gold on Marlboro 100's, a longer version of the king size smoke. A modified gold and white package introduced another extension, Marlboro Lights, to great success. Trends seemed to be drifting to "light" on everything from beer to potato chips, not to mention numerous well-received cigarette brands.

The cigarette brands that were launched as light (low tar and nicotine), such as True, Carleton, and Now, didn't have many options for expansion. They could hardly attempt to introduce a stronger, heavier brand. But Marlboro had no problem. From its full-flavored original to its longer length 100's to its Lights—and even a menthol version—the brand achieved solid success, acceptance, and number one status. Nothing could be better.

Well, maybe not.

Research was indicating that men, the traditional majority smokers, perceived the very popular Marlboro Lights gold and white package as being a bit feminine—good enough to smoke all right, but what about the rugged Marlboro man? The brand saw years of carefully honing its image as coming to a crossroad.

The answer: Marlboro Medium.

The new brand, in an only slightly modified version of the original red and white pack, and only slightly higher in tar and nicotine than Lights, told smokers the Man was back.

The smoking public responded with healthy sales figures for the new extension. Industry observers noted these guys didn't get to be, and to stay, number one by such a wide margin by not having the pulse of the marketplace. They built a brand and then built upon it with extensions for every taste within the brand parameters. As each of the versions are available in both soft pack and crush-proof box, there are (at least) ten ways to buy Marlboro.

And if you want to feel even better about your heart residing in Marlboro country, check the catalog of Marlboro brand clothing and related western fare. Being on the company's mailing list brings calendars with beautiful color photographs of the west, rugged and beautifully serene, as well as coupons for big discounts on cigarettes and even rebates for grocery money. That's to buy the fixin's for the treats described in the lavishly handsome, tall, lean, magnificent photo-illustrated piece *Marlboro Chuckwagon Cookin'—Twelve Authentic Recipes from Marlboro Country*. Leading with the phrase "A cowboy has an appetite ridin' a horse," the hearty recipies include the Tin Palate Special, Cowpoke Beans, Red Chili Biscuits, and Dried Apple Cakes, among others—images to delight even the most urban cowboy.

Marlboro kept a steady course. The brand's managers and advertising agency kept updating and enhancing their photography, discreetly even replacing their original Marlboro Man with a younger trailblazer, but always mindful of what ad people liked to call a big idea. They stayed with that idea, touching up the gray hairs, keeping it fresh, and treating it as a respectful stage on which newer versions of their product might be rolled out. Ironically, around 1954, Marlboro, a part of the new young group of filter cigarettes was perceived as more of a woman's brand. It too, has come a long way, baby—or cowboy, as the case may be.

Taking notice of the sentimental cliché "the old one's are the best," Marlboro in the 90s introduced "adventure team miles," basically a retooling of the trading stamp idea (used successfully some 40 years earlier by cigarette ancestor Raleigh). A catalog of "Marlboro adventure team gear," looking a lot like a scaled down version of the L.L. Bean catalog, shows camping gear, clothing, sport watches, and accessories—top quality and all branded with the Marlboro logo—available only for the coupons, on Marlboro cigarettes.

The Marlboro Adventure Team is an attempt to stretch Marlboro Country and the Marlboro Man across the rivers, rapids, and hills; beyond a western theme, but still remain bold and adventurous. It is also an attempt to have as many people as possible in the bold, adventurous 20-something, 30-something and the baby boomer demographic groups wearing, carrying, or otherwise displaying the Marlboro logo.

That is truly effective brand extension.

Camel

No discussion of cigarette marketing in the 1990s could overlook the case study of Camel, a brand that while seeming to have been around forever, projected a consistently contemporary image. In a regular size soft pack, unfiltered Camel was one of several mainstream male-oriented brands. Its package design ran somewhat counter to what modern image makers would have recommended: a profile of a camel (not historically among the most cuddly, attractive, or lovable beasts) in a desert setting. Deserts are hot and dry, two things cigarette manufacturers don't like to suggest as synonymous with their products. And yet, Camel did succeed and remained for decades a top brand, even when it was not spending in the same range as its much more widely advertised competition.

The brand also lacked a clearly defined comparative position in its category. While, for example, Newport and Salem used imagery of cool mountain streams and romantic young models, and Benson & Hedges offered a bit of snob appeal, Camel just suggested it was a quality tobacco product if you wanted one. Such an indefinite position succeeded here; whereas, it helped to sink rival brand Pall Mall.

In the 1950s nightly sponsorship of the evening news ("the Camel News Caravan with John Cameron Swayze")

From beach towels to bomber jackets and dozens of products in between, Camel uses branded merchandise, magazines, inserts, and outdoor ads, such as this one on the side of a downtown Chicago hotel, to introduce and promote its line extension that includes lights, special lights, ultra-lights and wides.

Chapter Five

and gift cartons of Camel sent free to U.S. servicemen made the brand of "fine Turkish tobacco" 100 percent American in the consumers' mind.

When smokers showed a preference for king size filter cigarettes, Camel accommodated. The brand extension didn't overwhelm the industry but held its own competitively, a solid, no-nonsense extension.

When the trend went to lights, Camel lights were launched very successfully, enjoying solid and steady sales. The "Camel Man," a rugged individual who appeared to be a product of the good life, was featured in several ads promoting Camel Lights. The cigarette did much better than the advertising, which proved quite forgettable.

In the 1980s the fourth member of the family was born, Camel Ultra-Lights—a still lower tar cigarette. And in the '80s as well Camel brought about the return of an advertising figure that would make the brand the talk of the town: Old Joe.

The cartoon illustrated camel was the centerpiece of the monumentally ambitious ad campaign that showed a very "cool Joe" in sunglasses and designer wardrobe on billboards, in magazines, in pop-up ads and point of sale displays . . . and on Camel bucks. Again, the concept behind the coupon on each pack was to collect and redeem them for merchandise from nightshirts to dart boards to denim jackets and sweatshirts. Premium catalogs were published in volumes. All merchandise carried the cool cartoon logo character in various poses.

Multiple-pack promotions included free t-shirts, fleece shorts, jackets—and free packs of cigarettes. And if all these choices didn't seem like aggressive enough marketing, Camel came up with another brand extension—Camel Wides. This thicker light cigarette had a uniquely different size and an appeal to smokers of cigarillos and small cigars (as more public places were discouraging or prohibiting cigar smoking).

And even while the jury was still out on the success of Camel Wides, the brand launched a head-on marketing assault on the top-selling Marlboro Lights with the introduction of Camel Special Lights. Camel may well have the largest (or, as they might prefer, *widest*) line extension of any cigarette brand in history.

The Wall Street Journal in an article on efforts by the R.J. Reynolds Tobacco Company to boost sales of its three core brands—Winston, Salem, and Camel—noted "Camel, the first beneficiary of RJR's marketing plan, has so far demonstrated the most success . . . The brand also has lured fresh recruits with the . . . introduction of Camel Wides and its Camel Cash program, which bestows items like baseball hats, jean jackets, and beach towels on Camel smokers.

"As a result, Camel has managed to steal some fire from best-selling Marlboro."

Camel cigarettes had introduced "The Camel Collection" of men's clothing and "The Camel Expeditions" travel tours. There are some who will argue that selling or giving away clothing, trips, or merchandise is a questionable way to sell cigarettes. Some, of course, will argue that the very idea of selling cigarettes—much less with the use of cartoon characters—should be revisited for a number of reasons. While the subject lends itself to controversy, as it has for generations, the fact remains that the tobacco industry is a highly competitive, multi-billion dollar industry in which the survivors must consistently demonstrate creativity and commitment. Again, the key components for success are reliable research and a well-defined marketing plan. For Camel to have five brands competing successfully suggests it knew its market, their tastes, lifestyles, and interests as well as their sensitivities (ultra-lights) and their sense of humor (a cartoon spokesbeast and wacky merchandise). The fact that the product gains in an atmosphere of controversy is testament to good product positioning, management, and marketing—and, most importantly, to knowing what the market wants.

In the final analysis, the marketplace decides the value of the product, as it should. If a product is positioned badly or is a bad product—no amount of advertising or promotion will keep it alive for very long. Between soft packs and "hard packs" (the brand's version of the crush-proof box) Camel cigarettes are offered in a dozen or so variations including regular, filter, lights, light 100's, ultra lights, wides, wide lights, Camel 99's lights, and Special Lights. With about $800 million in sales in 1992, it ranked fifth among cigarette brands but appeared to have the greatest number of brand extensions, virtually all regarded as successful.

Alas, one non-success: in 1992, Joe the Camel, through an elaborate campaign with buttons, stickers, posters, and paper napkins, plates, and cups, sought the presidency of the United States of America. While history books will likely not record the exercise for posterity, those who witnessed it—and collected the logo-emblazoned premiums—will remember old Joe remained "cool."

Sex Sells ... Sometimes

Playboy

Playboy is a brand name rich in imagery, the word having come to symbolize far more than the magazine from which an empire grew. *Playboy,* as a publication, defined the men's magazine category by combining beautiful photographs of beautiful women with a high level of quality in virtually everything else within its pages: top fiction writers, essayists, and sports columnists along with interviews with world leaders and deep thinkers. Even the ads in the publication were more elegant and sophisticated than appeared most elsewhere. The early ads that ran for the magazine itself appeared under a headline asking "What sort of man reads *Playboy?*"

The answer, it was suggested, was a youthful, yet mature, sophisticated, literate lover of the good life, who could afford, if not to live it, certainly to aspire to it. It was a classic example of the advertiser asking "Can you see yourself in this picture?" to an audience that resoundingly insisted it most definitely could. It succeeded spectacularly from its very start, achieving for itself a respect and respectiblity in a magazine category that literally had none. This was not another "men's magazine" with articles and photos of beautiful nude women. It was a philosophical manifesto.

But sometimes achieving great success can cause one's compass to go haywire, causing one to believe there is such a thing as a "golden touch."

Between branded products and licensing deals with a broad range of ventures in between, Playboy Enterprises learned the expensive lesson that everything to which it affixed the Playboy name (and suggested with it the Playboy persona) did not automatically succeed.

Playboy's founder and its original editor and publisher, Hugh M. Hefner, articulated and sought to embody "the Playboy philosophy" in his writings and lifestyle. Following the success of his magazine, he served as host of a television show "Playboy's Penthouse" and, later, "Playboy After Dark." While awkward and superficial, the TV programs tried to bring the glamour and sophistication of the magazine to life. They launched the beginning of *Playboy's* brand extension and Hefner's drive to put the name that he now thought represented a way of life on all things attendant to that way of life: A coast-to-coast chain of Playboy Clubs; members only night clubs featuring the top entertainers of the world; a book publishing company, Playboy Press, that offered upscale and pricey works on censorship, music, wine, and even *The Playboy Illustrated History of Organized*

Crime; a record label that specialized in jazz and, later, country music; and even a chain of Playboy Hotels.

These products—from magazines to hotels—could be considered brand extensions in that they used the same name and sought to capitalize on the same image and brand identification in the marketplace. They also operated fully under the same ownership and management that distinguishes the ventures as brand extensions, rather than as licensing.

Licensing was another avenue and one that Hefner exploited mightily in lucrative deals that put the Playboy name and its rabbit head symbol on clothing, glassware, jewelry, and a plethora of other merchandise including automobile air fresheners.

While some products and ventures were more successful than others, the public didn't expend much energy in scrutinizing the business side of the matter because it was, after all, Hefner's money and if he chose to indulge himself in being a publisher/filmmaker/hotelier/night club-owner, whose business was it?

But just as any notorious public misstep becomes the stuff of gossipy rise-and-fall legends—and Hefner had indeed become, if not a legend, at least a character much larger than life as head of the empire he created—the ears on the Playboy rabbit began to droop along with the company's revenue.

A couple of things happened.

The first was *the sexual revolution*. The late 1960s through the 1970s saw an atmosphere of openness and more liberal attitudes toward sex and sexuality. Nudity was acceptable—even routine—in major Hollywood films. National news magazines and "encounter groups" had people openly sharing their most intimate thoughts. In the midst of all this, the *Playboy* image seemed out of date and out of touch. The famous "bunnies" of the night clubs seemed dated, trussed up in harness-like skimpy outfits with rabbit

---

Brand Extension

ears and tails, when competing clubs were featuring topless or nude dancers for those who wanted that sort of diversion. The law of diminishing returns took over with a vengence.

The urban sophisticates were not just "the sort of men who read *Playboy*" but a growing group that included many unlikely men and a lot of high-profile, outspoken, assertive women, too.

The flagship magazine's sales declined dramatically and the nightclubs, still "members only," fell on hard times; it was out of place in the prevailing environment, positioned wrong for the times.

The second problem was that the smooth, smirking image of the "playboy" played fine in the early '60s, but with the rise of feminism, the clubs and hotels were out of step with the market. Few women felt comfortable going (even as someone's date) to the nightclub where waitresses dressed as "bunnies" and many business people felt that management would take a dim view of "the Playboy Hotel," with all the frivolous connotations, turning up on expense account reports.

What could have been an entire profitable empire going the way of the hula hoop was turned around by a series of events timely or coincidental. Hefner, while retaining his title of chairman, all but retired to his estate in California, succeeded by his bright, business-oriented—rather than image-oriented—daughter. A team of career business and management professionals moved into the executive offices. The clubs closed, hotels were sold or renamed, and the record company and book publishing companies disappeared. The film production company, after several disastrous large-budget movies, began concentrating on more modestly budgeted home video projects and programs for the company's fledgling cable television channel.

If a market observer would conclude *Playboy* had stumbled, it was for these reasons:

1. Failing to take the pulse of the market regularly to see if it was still giving the public what it wanted

2. Diversifying into areas where it made little or no sense to assume its name would carry weight

3. Indulging itself by thinking that because one person or team could put out a successful magazine, he or they could compete successfully in records, books, clubs, or hotels

By the early 1990s, *Playboy* was again doing well. The magazine was profitable and seemed to accept that it was a literate, sexy men's magazine and not a way of life. Magazine spin-offs were in the form of calendars, games, and collected pictorials (basically out-take photos) from the magazine itself. *Playboy* is enormously successful in home videos, which are virtually video versions of the magazine. It is too early to tell whether these videos can carry an entire cable TV operation very far into the future, but odds are about even.

Playboy remains determined to exploit its name and logo as best it can. This is best exemplified in a single collected place: a mail order catalog. "Playboy Products for Good Times" offers videos, lingerie, jewelry, and other merchandise as well as back issues of the magazine.

Although there clearly is a lot of money to be made in automobile air fresheners, *Playboy* seems to have returned to doing what it has historically done well and profitably. Career business executives now guide the corporation Hugh Hefner once ran on instincts. It is unlikely future ventures will stray too far afield. In May 1992, the company announced it was forming a custom publishing and database division in order to leverage the brand name of its flagship magazine and attract reluctant advertisers. The custom breakthrough allows advertisers to actually be in *Playboy* issues without photos of nude women, targeted to specific audiences. The cumulative result suggests that in modern times, even a playboy must check his bank balance occasionally and adjust.

Pretend You Know Me

American Express

Like *Playboy*, American Express is a brand not always thought of as a brand per se, but rather as a company—a very large company—involved in numerous businesses including banking, travel, mutual funds, brokerage, investment banking, publishing, and technology. In some cases, one must squint to find the American Express identification, so subtle is their desire for recognition. In other cases, like the most important movie stars, they proudly show their name above the title of their individual divisions. One might conclude this reflects a desire on the company's part to have it both ways, the kind of high visibility with successes that impress shareholders, while keeping a lower profile with the less profitable or more controversial units.

On one side, the American Express "green" card and American Express Travelers Cheques have historically brought the brand high visibility and prestige as well as revenue. Brand extensions such as the American Express "gold" card and Travel services have enhanced both image and profits. Indeed, the company entered the 1990s with $9.9 billion in revenues from travel related businesses alone, despite a significant decline in those revenues since the 80s.

With what some analysts might consider clearly an obvious success preordained for 1980s brand extensions, the "platinum" card (going the prestigious gold card one better) and the Optima card (to compete on a consumer level with rival bank cards Visa and Mastercard) both turned into disasters financially and major public embarrassments to the firm.

The platinum card was ill-conceived from the beginning. Even the most snobbish potential patron dismissed the idea of a card so class-conscious, one could not even apply for it, but must wait to be "invited" to receive it—and then pay a stiff annual fee for the "privilege" of using it.

Granted, the gold card was a big success and did afford a certain status. And granted too that as more gold cards came into circulation and more competitors offered their own versions (often at lower fees) the snob appeal diminished. But the case for the platinum card was such a weak one, so lacking in significant benefit, and launched in such a depressed economic cycle that it sank of its own weight.

One would have expected that American Express, with all its resources, would have learned from even the most superficial of research that it was offering a product the marketplace did not want and certainly did not need. What publicity the platinum card received was laced with ridicule.

The Optima card was a similar but different type of failure, though equally unjustifiable given the talent and resources of American Express. For years, American Express, Diners' Club, and Carte Blanche owned the charge card business. Customers—or *members,* as the companies preferred to call them— paid an annual fee and paid account balances in full each month. When the banks entered the business in the 1960s, ultimately consolidating a myriad of labels under the banners Visa and Mastercard, they employed the revolving charge system by which customers could pay installments on their balances each month, plus interest charges, and a smaller, if any, annual fee than asked by the big three. Given the huge number of banks sending cards unsolicited to their customers, it was only a matter of time before those customers asked why they needed the more costly three cards when the bank cards were so much cheaper and more accessible. How they responded can be summarized by noting American Express' share of the U.S. general-purpose charge business was 25 percent in the 1980s, 22.3 percent in 1990, and 20.6 percent in 1991, according to a report by *Advertising Age*.

Where had American Express cards fumbled?

They should have seen signs of trouble brewing when, in the late 1980s, with the U.S. economy in recession and concern about credit rising, merchants began complaining about (and many began refusing to honor) American Express cards because the merchant-paid service fees were so much higher than those of its competitors. The issue reached an extreme when a group of Boston merchants actually organized a boycott of the company, with accompanying national news coverage.

Not only didn't American Express budge on its service fees, but it continued to charge rates to "members" that were double or triple the annual fees charged by Visa and Mastercard participating banks.

During this time, Sears introduced the Discover card, yet another addition to the charge card derby, its only success in a large list of corporate misjudgments. Discover was rolled out with massive advertising and publicity support and positioned as versatile and highly benefit-weighted and value-oriented.

Both Visa and Mastercard increased their advertising, and Visa included a direct frontal assault, noting places of interest that welcomed the Visa card but would not accept American Express.

The American Express reaction was somewhere between arrogant and ineffectual. The company that had scored so well over the years with friendly, memorable effective advertising campaigns such as one using big name celebrities with unfamiliar faces asking "Do you know me?" or actor Karl Malden sounding the alarm for Travelers Cheques, ("Don't leave home without them") didn't seem inclined to dignify competitors' taunts with a response.

A very expensive American Express ad campaign during this period merely showed very famous people in elegant portrait photos, noting their names and how many years they'd been an American Express member.

With all due respect, while others are offering cost savings and convenience, telling people they might want to get an American Express card because Paul Newman, Wilt Chamberlain, and Rob Reiner have each had one for years isn't much of a case for value.

If the Optima card was to go head-to-head with the bank cards, someone should have told the Optima people.

Again, an ad program that seemed to say the main benefit to having this card was that it was from American Express lacked punch. Cost advantages relative to bank cards were not obvious. Promotion was heavily aimed at current AmEx members via direct mail solicitations, thus cannibalizing the core product somewhat, while failing to lure new converts.

Further, merchants did not respond to Optima with nearly the enthusiasm shown the Discover card or newer editions of Visa.

Where was the research?

Where was the unique selling proposition?

What about the discounts, rebates and a warm, inviting message instead of the detached air of one who really didn't need your business anyway?

With enormous competitive pressure increasing as General Motors, General Electric, Ford, and AT&T each promoted their entry into the market with customized Visa cards, American Express needed to react much more like an express and less like an overcrowded "local."

According to *Advertising Age,* American Express committed $1.1 billion in 1992 to marketing. A creative approach with a greater emphasis on value must re-energize the company's sagging core brands, the green card and the travelers cheques, while defining *added* value to consumers for the gold card, Optima card, and travel services. Even in a rebound economy, consumers and merchants will not pay high fees for the "privilege" of having an American Express card. The word privilege is shown in quotes because it starred in another unsuccessful American Express ad campaign, "Membership has its privileges."

Once again, the arrogance and snob appeal were wrong for a social and economic climate that did not endorse a privileged class. Additionally, the privilege suggested in the ads, namely insurance, was similar to that offered by competitors as well.

Survival, much less growth, of this division depends on a competitive fee structure and a message that speaks to value, not just status.

Another misstep for the firm was in the area of investing, and this was a *double* misstep in that a firm that wants to invest and manage other people's money should be more careful about how it so publicly handles its own. In many ways American Express has grown by innovation, but in recent years it has sought to grow by acquisition. Much of that has been in the highly visible investment and brokerage area.

IDS, founded in 1894 as Investors Diversified Services, is a Minneapolis-based financial services firm that had achieved considerable success, particularly in the mutual fund business, before being acquired by American Express in 1984. Well-managed with a fine sense of public interest, it was American Express' most profitable division in 1992, with posted assets under management of more than $65 billion, according to *Business Week.* So while it basked in the glow of prosperity and a good public image, American Express announced in 1993 that it would spend approximately $1 billion to redesign the operation over a four-year period. Its new name would be American Express Personal Financial Planning.

While the final determination of success or failure must be left to history, consider these two points:

1. In the minds of Wall Street analysts and public investors and consumers, American Express has blundered a few times, lost an enormous amount of money, and appears to qualify as a falling star.

2. IDS has a good public image and is enormously profitable. What good business sense does it make to dismantle it and reconfigure it under the name of a slipping brand?

The company could have launched a major high-profile advertising and publicity campaign that identified it proudly—boldly—as "IDS, an American Express Company" and left it to keep building and growing on its very solid foundation.

On another front, the company took an opposite approach.

Having acquired the brokerage firm from Shearson Hayden Stone in the 1970s, it changed the name to Shearson American Express. Then, upon acquiring the investment banking firm, Lehman Brothers, it changed the brokerage firm's name first to Shearson Lehman American Express, then just to Shearson Lehman, while having the investment banking unit operate as Lehman Brothers (with absolutely zero reference to American Express in its ads—even in the legal fine-print copyright information). By March of 1993, the company was talking about unloading the entire brokerage division and had indeed courted buyers publicly.

This would suggest that the company wants to identify itself with the IDS success (even adhere itself to it) and, perhaps, distance itself from the risky investment banking activities of Lehman Brothers. The message it sends to shareholders, analysts, and the general public, however, could suggest a rudderless ship.

Not widely known is the extent of American Express' involvement in publishing. At the end of 1992, the company owned and published the magazines *Travel & Leisure, Food & Wine, L.A. Style, D,* and *Atlanta.* If the firm wanted to position itself as the investment company, rather than as a publisher per se, fine . . . since early 1993 saw the announcement that by spring, 1993, management control of the magazines would pass from American Express to Time Warner.

If American Express had a plan, it was a hazy one.

What is it? What does it seek to be?

It can operate as many companies as it chooses under separate names, but they should be boldly identified as "An American Express Company" if the brand is to have value. Or the companies should all have names that take second place to the parent (American Express Food & Wine, American Express/IDS Personal Finance, American Express/Lehman Brothers, etc.). A company cannot maximize the exploitation of the value of its brand name if it shades or hides that brand name.

The public and the market are historically forgiving. If the firm "has its act together," a major public relations initiative should spell out the things it's doing right in newspaper and magazine "advertorials" and public appearances. The Mobil Oil Corporation used exactly this approach in the oil industry crisis in America and won respect, as well as recognition, for its candor, integrity, and strength.

American Express should be committed to enhancing the value intrinsic in its name. The marketplace will tell it if and when it reaches a point of no return. As confusion persists, American Express may appear in one of its own ads asking "Do you know me?"

Big Wheels from Out of Town

Honda

Honda's experience in the U.S. market is an example of need catching up to a product.

When Honda made its American debut, it was as a motorcycle ... a *small* motorcycle. The motorcycles Americans had related to up to that point were, for the most part, large and powerful machines such as Harley-Davidsons. State troopers rode these no-nonsense motorcycles. But the Honda motorcycle, like similar Japanese bikes made by Suzuki and Yamaha, was lightweight, smaller, economical, and easy to handle. It was also relatively inexpensive.

A significant distinction enters at this point: for years Japanese import products, from radios to copy machines, had pretty much been dismissed as cheap—both cheap to buy and cheaply made. Certainly, these "made in Japan" brands were vastly inferior to "American made" products. Honda (along with Sony, Panasonic, and a few others) changed the way Americans thought of Japanese products. As provincial as the American consumer chose to be at times, grudging recognition was paid to the fact that this new generation of Japanese products, particularly in motors and electronics, were equal to or better than their American counterparts in terms of quality and technology—and usually cost a lot less.

Honda became the motorcycle of choice for college and high school students in need of dependable, low cost transportation. The image grew of the male student in tweed jacket and necktie motorcycling across campus in a Honda.

As environmental interest grew and fuel economy became a larger concern, avoiding traffic jams and easily finding a place to park became more important considerations. Young executives joined their student brethren and turned in their cars for motorcycles, the most popular of which was Honda. So popular in fact, it was the subject of a pop song "Little Honda" that topped the record charts in 1964. As economical, basic transportation, the product had achieved clear niche respectability.

Then Honda took an extremely bold step: the motorcycle company tried to sell Americans cars.

The initial response was dismissive. Suggestions were that the company was putting those little motorcycle tires on, well, little cars and didn't deserve to be taken seriously. The price was small too and, relative to the cost of an American-made car, seemed to suggest it had to be a "cheap" product. Then two things happened. The first was that the cars performed well in terms of fuel-efficiency, dependability, and maintenance. The second was the social trend shift that attacked "big, expensive gas guzzlers" and embraced small, economical cars.

The Honda tires got a little bigger, and so did the passenger compartment. While in no danger of being mistaken for an Oldsmobile, Honda had fine-tuned its car to the point where its Civic became a top seller, a symbol of fuel efficiency and good engineering.

If the brand extension leap from motorcycle to motor car wasn't impressive enough, in the 1980s, Honda introduced Accura, a line of luxury cars with features, appointments, and performance on a par with established luxury cars. The Honda name does not appear on the car or in its advertising, lest the consumer have second thoughts about paying luxury prices for ... a Honda.

From motorcycle to family car to luxury car, Honda looked at what people wanted in transportation and created and sold quality products that met that need. The brand's advertising was consistent and direct, keeping its profile—and the product's benefits—high. It was a simple approach, and it succeeded.

Hyundai

Much of this work has focused on recommendations for choosing the right name, positioning yourself clearly, and striving for familiarity and recognition so that the "brand power" of a core product can be comfortably transferred to benefit another product. Here Hyundai runs into trouble.

The brand entered the United States in 1986 with considerable fanfare, a large ad budget—and a compact car—the Hyundai Excel. As word spread throughout the automobile industry that Hyundai was coming in strong and planning to become a major force fast, surprisingly (given its history) the industry took the threat seriously.

Alas, according to the trade publication *Automotive News*, Hyundai Motor America entered the 1990s with somewhere around one percent of U.S. car and light truck sales, having apparently peaked in 1988 when a record 264,282 units were sold.

As compact cars go—import or domestic—Hyundai came in with a very competitive and respectable product in terms of quality, design, style, performance and, above all, price. It entered the U.S. market, too, at a time when the American auto industry did nothing to discourage import bashing, particularly the disparaging of cars made in Japan.

Hyundai cars are products of South Korea, but that was a relatively minor distinction in that the brand made little effort to distance itself from Japanese imports. Toyota, Nissan, Honda, and Subaru were holding an increasingly large market share in spite of strong "buy American" advertising.

The simple fact was that these imports were generally cheaper—or at least cost competitive—and represented a greater value in terms of performance, quality, style, and engineering. This did much to blunt the hoped-for swell of patriotic sentiment. American consumers apparently preferred to choose their battles. Clearly some folks would always only buy American, but on such big ticket items as cars, consumers were more interested in value than dressing in the flag. Consumers candidly charged that Detroit had let them down. In such a climate, a new and considerably lower- priced import should have done spectacularly, but Hyundai:

1. As the newest player in a crowded field had to work a lot harder and spend more for recognition.

2. Found American consumers hesitant, with a lack of knowledge about how Korean-made cars measured up against Japanese, much less American cars.

3. After more than five years in the U.S. market, couldn't get people to say (much less spell) the brand's name correctly. Hyundai rhymes with Sunday. Yet announcers even in their own commercials might say "High-Yun-Dye."

Heading toward the twenty-first century, Hyundai appeared to be serious about establishing itself as a brand of foreign car in the U.S., albeit with a modest share of the market. As its identification with the compact family car market was building, the company introduced the upscale Sonata, the sporty Scoupe, and the subcompact Elantra— three models with very differing levels of appeal—a questionable move for a brand that still needed to define itself.

But cars having different models is not a defenseless position, despite the brand's youth. What is terribly odd is the introduction of the Hyundai personal computers to the U.S. market at a time when the autos were still an unpronounceable brand to many.

One would expect that well-financed non-U.S. companies would do considerable research before entering a new market. Hyundai certainly had the resources to do so, and their products could stand up well under scrutiny. Yet Hyundai did not define its unique selling proposition for its cars and did so even less for its computers. Both were in the low single digits in market share in the 1990s. The marketer's message must give consumers a *reason* to buy. It's not enough to just be there.

The Candy Wars

Think of Valentine's Day, Mother's Day, Sweetest Day, Secretary's Day, birthdays, anniversaries, and a little something for the hostess ... and it's likely candy comes to mind. When there's no particular occasion at all, candy is still very big business—a $6.4 billion business, according to Nielsen Marketing Research and *Advertising Age*. In 1992, Hershey foods dominated with a 26.6 percent share of the U.S. market. Its closest competitor, M&M/Mars had a 23.9 percent share for the same period. That these two companies sell half of all the candy sold annually in the United States suggests the obvious power in production and distribution, but it also suggests that they both have a very good sense of what keeps America's sweet tooth sweet. They are intensely competitive, alert to not only the changing range of tastes, but of convenience considerations—from"bite size" to family packs—and even status (Hershey's Golden Almond Bar in its elegant gold foil wrap is selling an upscale image as much as it's selling good chocolate); Snickers proudly proclaims it was the "official snack food of the U.S. Olympic Team."

How much of America's favorite sweets are Hershey's or M&M/Mars, and how intense is the competition to make each brand within brand work harder? Start with this list (for purposes of illustration, we've concentrated on major confectionery brand products):

Hershey's at Your Candy Counter Now

Hershey's milk chocolate bar

Hershey's milk chocolate w/almonds

Hershey's Dark chocolate bar

Hershey's Cookies & Mint chocolate bar

Hershey's Big Block Bar

Hershey's Miniatures

Hershey's Kisses

Hershey's Mr. Goodbar

Hershey's Krackel bar

Hershey's Giant Kiss

Hershey's Golden Almond Bar

Hershey's Golden Almond Solitaires

Reese's Peanut Butter Cup

Reese's Miniatures

Reese's Pieces

Reese's Crunchy Peanut Butter Cup

Almond Joy

Mounds

Skar toffee bar

Whatchamacallit bar

Symphony candy bars

York Peppermint Pattie

5th Avenue bar

Kit Kat bar

Rolo

. . . and in the dairy case at the grocery store

Hershey's Free (chocolate pudding)

Hershey's chocolate drink

Hershey's chocolate drink mix

Hershey's flavored drinks

M&M/Mars Sweet Selections

M&M's chocolate candy

M&M's peanut chocolate candy

M&M's almond chocolate candy

M&M's peanut butter candy

Mars Milky Way bar

Mars Dark Chocolate Milky Way bar

Mars Milky Way II (reduced fat) candy bar

Milky Way ice cream bars

Milky Way Milk shakes

Mars Almond Bar

PB Max

Twix bar

Snickers bar

Snickers peanut butter bar

Snickers ice cream bars

3 Musketeers bar

3 Musketeers ice cream bars

Kudos

Holidays

Starburst

Skittles

Dove chocolate bars

Dove ice cream bars

Dove bite-size ice cream snacks

Hershey's

Some might make the case that candy is responsible for fortunes being made in dentistry and medicine as well as food products, but those are the people who probably don't have much fun. Some, of course, would argue that it doesn't deserve to be called "food."

The confectionery industry, large and powerful, even has its own trade association, The National Confectionery Association, and why shouldn't it, with the billions of dollars spent annually on candy? Perhaps the most popular candy is chocolate and some who would proudly declare themselves as "chocoholics" will vigorously debate the merit of Swiss chocolate versus German chocolate, of Godiva versus the Hershey bar, and of regional favorites from San Francisco's Ghirardelli to Chicago's Fannie May.

Certain old movies even suggested that World War II might have ended sooner if our fighting GIs had been able to hand out more coveted American chocolate bars to the excited Europeans, who treated the commodity with great reverence. In those days, "the Hershey bar" was a simple, basic, milk chocolate treat. As time went on and personal wealth increased, special treats became regular snacks, the Hershey bar added almonds (to start with), and snack food competitors recognized a good thing when they saw it.

Since the purpose of this volume is to examine brand-building methods, brand equity, and line extension, a lot of time should not be devoted to the history of chocolate (which reportedly came to our attention via the explorer Hernando Cortez about 400 years ago—after he'd heard about it from the Aztec Indians). We should instead focus on the heirs of the legacy of Milton Hershey and other marketers who have positioned the product and adapted it to changing times and changing tastes to maintain both position and profitability.

In 1992 Hershey Foods Corporation spent nearly $300 million to advertise its products. While this in itself may not appear unusual for a campaign with worldwide sales of more than $2 billion, it is in marked contrast to the 1960 article in *Sales Management* titled "How is Hershey Doing—Without Advertising?" The answer at the time was "doing well."

Clearly, 1960 was a long time ago.

In that article a Hershey executive prophetically said, "Please make it clear that we have no quarrel with advertising . . . The time will come when Hershey becomes an advertiser."

The company followed a philosophy that it has credited with building its operation to its great level of success: make a good product, sell it at the lowest possible price, and do some promotional work with retailers and distributors.

The philosophy is simple enough, but the marketing savvy the company has shown over the years demonstrates it has kept its finger on the public pulse.

First, the Hershey chocolate brand responded with a range of sizes from the standard size ("nickel") candy bar to opposite extremes, with both miniatures (bite size pieces, individually wrapped) to a large size bar that is the physical equivalent of five regular bars.

Next, it extended to meet the changing tastes by introducing such variations as dark chocolate and cookies & mint milk chocolate. The gold-foil wrapped Golden Almond bar and Golden Almond Solitaires met the image requirements of the 1980s baby boomers who had expressed a blatant desire to buy upscale everything, from gourmet coffee beans to candy bars.

Additionally, as the 1980s and '90s brought a broader range of beverage alternatives (including flavored coffees, flavored teas, fruit-flavor colas and an increasing cross-mixing of fruit juices with plain or carbonated water), Hershey was not to be left out. Having already introduced the "chocolate drink" with some modest success in grocers' dairy cases, the brand added three new extensions: Hershey's Banana Split, Hershey's Strawberry Drink, and Hershey's Chocolate Marshmallow Drink. Further, two points reflecting very much the mood of the times, each container carried a miniature "farm" logo and the words "naturally delicious" and the packaging itself was a wax-like coated paper box—more "environmentally friendly" than the plastic or glass containers of other beverages.

While its corporate finger was on the pulse of the baby boomers, it remembered its other constituent groups with logical market segment derivative products, including Hershey's chocolate flavor syrup, Hershey's toppings, and Hershey's chocolate milk mix.

Hershey is a corporate giant that understands acquisition, diversification, and the fact some products aren't necessarily helped by sharing the name of a famous chocolate bar. Consequently, the Hershey Pasta Group is made up of eight regional brands: American Beauty, Delmonico, Light 'N Fluffy, Perfection, P&R, San Giorgio, Skinner, and Ronzoni. Most of these brands began the 1990s by outpacing their category in growth and by showing enormous potential to keep growing.

One of the more dramatic, yet logical, stretches into diversification came when Hershey extended the line of its extremely popular Reese's peanut butter cups to include a crunchy variation as well as Reese's miniatures, Reese's peanut butter chips and, most logical of all, Reese's peanut butter cookies and . . . Reese's peanut butter!

Sensitive to health trends and the villainy often attributed to sweets, the company continues to pursue low fat, low calorie versions of its products.

As public taste moved to premium class, low cal, fruit flavors—and pasta—Hershey fortunately had the financial resources as well as the distribution capabilities to respond aggressively. It also had clout, developed over more than 90 years in business under the same name, a *brand* name, carefully nurtured and stretched.

M&M/Mars

M&M/Mars, according to the trade magazine *Advertising Age*, has "been on a mission to reclaim its lead in the U.S. candy galaxy and with an array of new products is closing in on leader Hershey Chocolate U.S.A."

That comment could have been made at almost anytime during the 1980s, as the two candy giants tried constantly to "one-up" each other with new brand extensions and product acquisitions.

Under the Mars, Inc. corporate flag are such successful brands as Uncle Ben's Rice, Uncle Ben's cooking sauces, Kal

In two-pound bags or mini-packs and numerous sizes in between, M&M's candies continue to offer not just a size, but a taste for every taste—plain chocolate, peanut, almond, peanut butter, and chocolate mint. The brand is highly aggressive in its extension strategy.

Kan pet foods, Whiskers cat food, Sheba cat food, and Pedigree dog food.

M&M's bite size candies were a long-time favorite, but the peanut butter filled extension, in a bright red version of the famous brown wrapper, was also an instant success. In the late 1980s food marketers launched a virtual peanut butter explosion, and M&M's was in the thick of it.

Snickers, for many years America's most popular candy bar, introduced its own peanut butter version.

Perhaps the most closely watched extension was the Milky Way II. With 25 percent fewer calories than its popular parent bar, it was the first reduced fat, reduced calorie bar in the M&M/Mars stable. Nearly six years in development to match the flavor of Milky Way, the extension product aimed to meet the concerns of candy-loving health-conscious consumers.

In "The Sweet Truth About Confectionery," a pamphlet issued by the National Confectioners Association, the industry group attacks what it describes as "myths" that have created misunderstanding among consumers. "Candy can complement your healthy and active life style," an industry spokesperson told *The Wall Street Journal*.

Added David Leibowitz, a candy industry analyst with American Securities Corp., "You'd really prefer to eat the Milky Way II because of the lower calorie count and other nutritional benefits. The hard part, if you're a true confection fanatic, is the real Milky Way is notoriously better." Obviously, this issue is of great concern to nutritionists who have railed against sweets for generations.

Yet, the industry takes the approach of giving the public what it wants, and the public clearly has made its feelings known. According to a 1992 survey by *Candy Marketer Magazine*, 87 percent of store buyers participating said they expect sales of sugar-free products to increase over the next five years. The same survey reported that 43 percent of the stores that carry sugar-free candy indicated there was a need to have more sugar-free candy on the market.

The bold move by M&M/Mars into the extension area with modified Milky Way, multi-flavored Snickers, M&M's, and an assortment of candy bar flavored ice cream treats is in itself notable for a company regarded as conservative.

Like Hershey, M&M/Mars has the resources to be bold. Sales for the U.S. candy division alone were over $1.5 billion in 1992. And candy is one area where a brand can gain consumers' favor by promoting variety. If consumers had rejected a peanut butter flavored Snickers bar, it is unlikely that the core brand Snickers bar would have suffered great or lasting damage, if any at all. Some years earlier, the company had offered a candy bar called "Forever Yours" which it positioned as basically a Milky

Way with a dark chocolate coating in place of milk chocolate. The product never achieved much in the way of sales and was eventually dropped.

In some respects, it might seem there was considerable lack of forethought here. First, candy manufacturers know that the market for dark chocolate is considerably smaller than for milk chocolate. Second, the name "Forever Yours" was not a name that consciously or unconsciously had much appeal to male candy lovers; hence, the bar appeared positioned to appeal to the female side of the market—and older ones at that. The name Milky Way itself implies *milk* chocolate, too. And finally, the brand never received a fraction of promotional support that Milky Way or Snickers received. Ultimately, the brand just faded away.

In 1992 Mars introduced Dark Chocolate Milky Way, and the industry assumption is that it will do okay in its niche. In the same year, Hershey introduced Hershey's Special Dark Chocolate bar. While the company had long included a dark chocolate offering in its variety pack of miniature bars, this was the first time the flavor had come into its own prominence on the counter, both as a niche-appeal product and as an extension against the Dark Chocolate Milky Way. These two companies have the distribution machinery, promotional budgets, and retailer clout to match each other product for product, flavor for flavor, and extension for extension. It may not be *war* exactly, but it is competition at its most aggressive. Even in the worst economic times, people buy candy in all flavors and sizes, to the tune of billions.

Do candy makers attempt to apply their marketing savvy by reflecting the mood of the marketplace with such touches as "the Big Bar," "The Gold Bar," the sugar-free alternative snack bar, and even timely and trendy tributes like the ill-fated "Reggie Bar" (for baseball hero Reggie Jackson)? Absolutely.

In the case of "Reggie," few people ever really expected it to achieve the status of its baseball predecessor Baby Ruth (which one line of folklore claims was created to honor "The Babe"). But Hershey expects to sell a lot of its Special Dark Chocolate, in no small part because they've dubbed it "special," recognizing that the term "special blend" has helped sales of products from coffee to cat food.

Companies with the resources of Hershey and M&M/Mars can afford to take some risks, but smaller or more conservative companies will want to treat new entries or reentries into the crowded candy counter display with the same considerations as might apply to most other industries, starting with research.

When extending a brand, determine first *what* the public wants in terms of size, shape, or flavor—if indeed it wants the product at all. If you are so sure that what you've got is so good—or better than the rest—and that the public will find it irresistible, test it. While research is essential to the successful launch and positioning of virtually any product, it is especially valuable in the food product category.

A really good marketer might be able to induce the public to come back for another try with a promise that "this year's model is faster than last year's model" or that the product "now gets your clothes even whiter" but people will long remember—and tell their friends about—a product that doesn't taste good.

Test it. Research will save costly missteps and it is the kind of shrewd marketing dollar allocation even the penny-wise Martin Hershey would deem worthy.

The Now Famous Cola Wars

One reason so much of this section has been devoted to "the cola wars" is that in Coca-Cola and Pepsi-Cola all the elements exist for what might be called the classic textbook case: fiercely aggressive competitors, solid equity in both brands with strong core products, failed brand extensions, hugely successful brand extensions, corporate politics, and some of the most successful and memorable advertising in history.

Coca-Cola and Pepsi-Cola are forever linked in the minds of consumers and, indeed, professionals in virtually every industry, as the most famous competitors in America—if not the world. More than GM and Ford, or NBC and CBS, or the Democrats and the Republicans, Coke and Pepsi have made their battle to be number one as famous as their incredibly successful beverages themselves.

In 1991 PepsiCo, parent company of Pepsi-Cola, ranked fifth on *Advertising Age*'s list of the 100 Leading National Advertisers. PepsiCo's ad spending was listed at $903.4 million. The Coca-Cola Company ranked twenty-eighth, spending a mere $367.4 million in comparison. Since PepsiCo is a larger operation with more divisions and operating units, a more cola-to-cola look at ad spending might be more representative of the battlefield. On their flagship brand's advertising, Coke spent $58 million to Pepsi's $61 million.

Why so competitive when, after all, it's only soda pop?

Coca-Cola's 1991 sales were $11.57 billion, PepsiCo's $19.6 billion. So the battle rages on, as it has for several generations now, with that word "generation" itself playing an important part in both the initial positioning of the brands and their ever-growing number of extensions.

Richard D. Harvey, president of the Seattle-based consulting firm Sound Marketing Services, took the two companies to task in a 1992 *Advertising Age* piece. Noting that cola growth appeared stalled in food stores (down almost 4 percent over an eight-year period), Mr. Harvey charged "They have failed to build real value and equity in their brands, turning instead to massive price-cutting backed by enormous advertising budgets featuring little more than star-studded irrelevancies."

While marketers and the public might long debate the return on multi-million dollar fees to "star-studded irrelevancies" featuring Michael Jackson, Ray Charles, Madonna, and Elton John, the phrase "failed to build real value and equity in the brands" is hardly descriptive of two of the most powerful, recognizable, profitable brands in history. In fact, a 1990 Lander Associates' Image Power Survey chart shown in *Adweek's* "Superbrands 1990" ranked Coca-Cola as number one on its list of "the Most Powerful Brands in the World." Pepsi-Cola ranked tenth in the survey. Of "The Most Powerful Brands in the U.S." Coca-Cola was also ranked number one; Pepsi-Cola was number four.

With such power and prominence comes controversy. For all the muscle at the supermarket, convenience store, or soda fountain these two companies may exert, their every new product test or advertisement comes under the kind of intense scrutiny and criticism normally accorded Broadway openings and tax reforms. And neither company has been above tossing the type of zingers at the other that one usually associates with schoolyard rivals.

Coca-Cola

Coca-Cola is the world's best-selling soft drink and that rare product surrounded by folklore, having its origins reported to be everything from a heavy-duty narcotic to a paint remover. Its formula is a more closely guarded secret than most bank vault combinations. A reliable source offers that the beverage was invented by a 53-year-old Georgia druggist named John Pemberton in 1886. When a chap named Willis Venable accidentally substituted carbonated water for Mr. Pemberton's plain water, Coca-Cola was officially born

Coca-Cola is not only perhaps the best-known brand name in the world, but can claim its "Coca-Cola Classic" deserves its name, having been brought back by popular demand after the company tried to retire it in favor of a "new Coke." (Courtesy of the Coca-Cola Company. Used with permission.)

as a soda fountain drink and by 1904 was being advertised in national magazines.

The brand building had begun.

Professor Richard S. Tedlow of the Harvard Graduate School of Business Administration recounts a speech by Mr. Harrison Jones, a Coca-Cola Company vice president and director of sales in the 1920s, in which the company is described as relentless in its desire for market research. Mr. Jones exhorted his sales force to "Know thy customers ... Know them intimately. Know them well. Have a daily tab on them ... If a record of purchases is kept tabulated at all times, daily, in your office, you, yourself, or your sales manager has constantly at hand a record of what every customer is doing and, above all, a record of what he is not doing. It is the pulse of your business, and the only way to feel the pulse of your entire business at one time. It enables you to intelligently analyze and to describe and to prescribe remedies."

Brand extension and promotions are not new to Coca-Cola. Records dating back to the 1920s have sales representatives fanning out across their assigned territories, loaded down with trunks of advertising materials, complimentary tickets, and circulars. While attempting to sell Coca-Cola fountain syrup, they would also offer for sale Coca-Cola chewing gum, cigars, and glasses bearing the Coca-Cola trademark. The glasses outsold the chewing gum and cigars.

As the company moved along from only selling syrup to bottling and selling Coca-Cola itself to selling bottling franchises, innovations and refinements continued, such as the handy, carry-home six-bottle carton of the early 1920s. The company was also spending more than a million dollars a year on advertising.

According to Professor Richard Tedlow, "everyone knew from the start that advertising would play a big role in this product's future. Coca-Cola advertising was designed not only to sell the product to the end consumer, but also to defend Coke against the many charges that it contained a dangerous amount of cocaine, alcohol, or caffeine."

Some insight into the company's idea of product positioning might be gained from this advertising copy, as it appeared in the July, 1905, issue of the national magazine the *Delineator*, as provided by Professor Tedlow, from the Coca-Cola Archives:

> Coca-Cola is a Delightful, Palatable, Healthful Beverage. It Relieves Fatigue and Is Indispensable for Business and Professional Men Students, Wheelmen and Athletes Relieves Mental and Physical

Exhaustion and Is the Favorite Drink for Ladies
When Thirsty, Weary, Despondent.

Not only did the product do a lot, so did its advertising. By 1913 the company claimed to have produced five million lithographed signs, as well as 200,000 cutouts for window displays; 50,000 metal signs for tacking under windows; two million trays for soda fountains; and numerous other items from calendars to baseball cards and pencils.

Coca-Cola was everywhere—a household word in the United States and around the world. And a household word at restaurants and concession stands (fountain sales still being an enormous component of Coke sales). The phrase ". . . and a coke" after the words hot dog, hamburger, popcorn, or most anything else, was commonplace. While McDonald's fast-food restaurants' well-known sign notes how many billion burgers have been sold, Coca-Cola, from as far back as 1917, has been advertising how many million a day had enjoyed a Coke. By the 1950s even small children could repeat along with the television announcer:

> Fifty million times a day,
> At home, at work, or on the way,
> There's nothing like a Coca-Cola
> Nothing like a Coke.

Coca-Cola has been fortunate in having leadership over the years that if not always visionary was at least competent. They had their share of hard times, but survived. Clearly the most influential force in the company's history was Robert W. Woodruff, who became president of Coca-Cola in 1923 and ran the company almost until his death at age 95 in 1985. A salesman and something of a showman, Mr. Woodruff would accept changes in packaging or changes in distribution, but one thing he vowed never to change was the basic core product, Coca-Cola, which he regarded as an institution. Acknowledging that the company had unsuccessfully tried its hand at brand extension around 1900 (Coca-Cola chewing gum and Coca-Cola cigars), Mr. Woodruff insisted that no further deviance or dilution of the core product or its name would occur, and so it was until his retirement in 1981. That year Diet Coke was introduced with great success. Mr. Woodruff did not live to see the introduction of the product New Coke, the creation of which he most certainly would have opposed.

The Coke name carried about as much clout in the marketplace as one could hope for. Management, particularly Robert Woodruff, had emphasized the importance in building and maintaining the value—the equity—of the Coke name.

But the 1980s was a time of increased concern about health and fitness, which went from fad to trend, with an explosion of often expensive and very successful nutrition books, exercise videos, health clubs, audio tapes—even the music and wardrobe to go with it. And sweet syrupy cola beverages were being passed over in favor of fruit juices, teas, or bottled water—until the industry caught on and offered sugar-free cola drinks. They were rarely as satisfying or flavorful as their sugary originals, but the public experimented with sacrifice and bought into the idea.

Coke's entry into the diet cola business was with Tab, a reflection of Mr. Woodruff's insistence that the Coca-Cola name belonged only on Coca-Cola. Despite its having the small print line "a product of Coca-Cola Company" on its packaging, Tab technically didn't qualify as a brand extension—nor should it have, considering its taste and packaging did nothing to suggest Coca-Cola. The product did fairly well, but never drew anywhere near the interest or sales figures of the parent company's flagship product.

So it was literally with the retirement of Robert Woodruff and the subsequent dawning of a new philosophy that the Coke name was unconstrained to enter a period of great expansion and extension.

The introduction of Diet Coke was not so much a product launch as a media event, with some 6,000 invited guests gathering at New York's Radio City Music Hall with singer Bobby Short, the Radio city Rockettes, and a 40-piece orchestra. A 14-foot can of Diet Coke rose on cue from the orchestra pit. The event was filmed, and the highlights were incorporated into the first Diet Coke commercial to underscore the importance of the event.

Not only did Diet Coke rapidly become the third largest-selling soft drink in the United States—and the nation's leading diet soft drink—but it was awarded the designation "Brand of the Decade" by the editors of *Advertising Age*.

Coca-Cola's first foray into true brand extension was more than a success, it was the stuff of product marketing history. Bolstered by this success and its sense of changing public tastes in which consumers seemed to be focusing on a desire for more and greater choices in virtually every area, the company embarked on a serious brand extension program that by 1985 would change the way people thought of Coke. Consumers could choose from a soft drink menu that included Coca-Cola, Caffeine-Free Coke, Diet Coke, Caffeine-Free Diet Coke, and Cherry Coke, as well as the company's non-cola drinks such as Sprite (to try to draw market share from 7-Up), Mr. Pibb (to draw market share from Dr. Pepper), flavored sodas under the Fanta label and, still hanging in, but well under the shadow of Diet Coke, Tab.

Coca-Cola had succeeded in responding to changing public tastes and moods and, in so doing, retained its worldwide preeminence as the choice among soft drinks.

But no review of the company's brand management or marketing strategy can overlook what will be debated as either the greatest exercise in corporate misjudgment or the greatest publicity stunt of modern times: the introduction of New Coke.

An article in *The Wall Street Journal* titled "New Coke Shows the Risks of Research" began, "When the Coca-Cola Company uncorked its new formula in April, 1985, executives boasted it was the surest move they had ever made. They described as 'overwhelming' the results of taste tests with 190,000 consumers, the majority of whom preferred the new recipe over the old Coke. By now, of course, everyone is well aware that it wasn't a sure thing."

Despite the broad dissemination of the adage "If it ain't broke, don't fix it," the Coca-Cola Company announced it would alter the taste of the world's best-selling soft drink.

The short reason for this apparently insane move was that rival Pepsi-Cola was gaining on Coke in market share. This new formulation, it was expected, would appeal to Pepsi drinkers, while still being Coke to Coke drinkers.

While the successful introduction of Diet Coke in Radio City Music Hall was a hard act to follow by anyone's standards, the advance word was that the Coca-Cola Company, on April 23, 1985, would offer security analysts and the press "the most important announcement in the company's ninety-nine year history."

Thomas L. Harris, public relations consultant and associate professor of corporate public relations at the Medill School of Journalism, Northwestern University, recounted that, "Hundreds of reporters and analysts attending in a theater in Lincoln Center learned about the reformulation of Coca-Cola. Media headlines made the world aware of "New Coke" overnight, touching off an immediate and negative reaction. The "New Coke," the now legendary product failure, reminded people how much they loved the old Coke, and put it back on top. Donald Keough, Coca-Cola's president, said that, "all the time and money and skill poured into market research on the new Coca-Cola could not measure or reveal the deep and abiding emotional attachment to

Coca-Cola." Professor Harris goes on to quote Mr. Keough as saying, "Some critic will say Coca-Cola made a marketing mistake. Some cynic will say that we planned the whole thing for the publicity value. The truth is that we are not that dumb and we are not that smart."

The experience continues to fascinate in part because there was little apparent reason to change the product initially. Why change when you're number one? And blaming market research for such a huge negative reaction seemed a bit of a stretch on two counts: First, who, with a straight face, would have ever looked for or characterized anyone as having a "deep and abiding emotional attachment" to a soft drink? And yet, secondly, researchers *are* skilled in reading "emotional" reactions and it's hard to believe that, out of 190,000 tests, no evidence whatsoever surfaced of such an intense feeling.

Most significantly, though, is the fact that "being smart" isn't related to just getting all the publicity. It is in being able to reintroduce your original product with, perhaps for the first time in advertising and marketing history, a truly legitimate claim to the phrase "back by popular demand" and to use the word "classic" on your product with pronounced justification, rather than its only having the appearance of a reformulated brand extension. "Classic," it is safe to suggest, is a much more powerful term than "the original formula."

Many marketers, though, believed Coke should have let the matter drop while they were ahead. They still had the "New Coke" on the market to appeal to Pepsi lovers, and now they had "Coke Classic." Classic racked up great sales and, while the figures weren't spectacular, the company *did,* in fact, sell a fair amount of New Coke. Imagine then the surprise, particularly on the part of those true believers who seriously believed that the company had simply made a mistake, when Coca-Cola announced in March 1990, that it planned to reintroduce New Coke under the name "Coke

II" with new packaging, to test markets prior to a national reintroduction.

Apparently pleased with the two-year test run in Spokane, Washington, the company plugged Coke II into Chicago outlets with a huge TV ad campaign, including a competitive ad taking aim at Pepsi. With not much of an attempt at subtlety, the ad copy read: "Real cola taste, plus the sweetness of Pepsi."

How effective was this frontal assault on the competition? According to an *Advertising Age* "ad test," less than a quarter of the people who saw the commercial could replay it. The trouble might have involved overlooking one of the basic elements of good, effective advertising. Where was the "unique selling proposition"—the USP? The ad test appraisal was that "Coke II may have a problem in that what's being communicated—a new name—isn't persuading soft drink purchasers to buy the product."

Consumers may *try* a product because of its name, but it's a little off the mark to assume that after they have rejected it they will try it again just because you've changed the name and sought a repositioning,

How is it that a company so savvy, that was almost obsessed with collecting research data in its early years, now looked to blame research for a past product's failure? Additionally, a smart marketer, with a lot of research and testing, apparently failed to learn what a trade magazine test easily determined—that its ad was not all that persuasive.

Whether called New Coke or Coke II, this product clearly stands to be a continuing embarrassment to the Coca-Cola Company. A cardinal rule in brand extension strategy is that the potential for negative reflection on the core brand should be held to a minimum. Obviously, a product called Coke II can hardly distance itself or disassociate with the core brand, Coke. It *can* take a niche marketing approach and focus on certain of its characteristics, such as it's sweeter so it's not for every taste. In that sense, if the extension (ahem!) fizzles, it might be dismissed on the basis of its niche characteristics (too small, too young, etc.) rather than leaving a residue that could stain the core product.

Taking on Pepsi with a guns-blazing, confrontational campaign is bold and might work if it carried a benefit (tastes better, lower cost, fewer calories, larger size . . .), but an attack without a clear reason for anyone to want you to win seems ill-conceived.

Unfortunately, as sales of Coke Classic hold their own and Diet Coke rise, Coke II is likely to be a continuing reminder that everything with the Coke name on it isn't necessarily something consumers want or will accept.

In January 1993, Coke again went head-to-head with Pepsi on a brand extension, although this time it seemed to be trying to learn something from its Coke II experience. When Pepsi, responding to public interest in things that at least *looked* pure, introduced a new clear beverage it called Crystal Pepsi (and Diet Crystal Pepsi), Coke responded with Tab Clear.

While Pepsi told the industry that it believed the "clear colas" provided a positive complement to their existing products and "broadens the appeal of our trademark," Coke has held back, perhaps even unwittingly undercutting its Tab product by vehemently insisting there will never be a clear Coca-Cola. Further, while both Pepsi and Diet Pepsi have mainstream appeal, Tab has long had an image in the marketplace as a soft drink for women on diets. The jury is still out on whether "clear colas" will make the grade, fade away, or become a huge bomb. In their "Cola wars" Coke and Pepsi appear to recognize that in these times of instant international news dissemination and broad interest in winners and losers, what's at stake is more than a cola. An evening television news story that one product or another has left its competition in the dust can mean not only the sales success and image enhancement that comes with being the winner, it can determine the price and direction of the company's stock. Coca-Cola cannot afford too many perceived misjudgments or ill-positioned product launches before its stockholders react in the same way those of any other large corporation would, exhorting management to get it right or get lost.

The Coca-Cola experience in brand building and brand extension may well be the example of the best and the worst. The "most powerful brand in the world," with a franchise that is perhaps the most recognized from Atlanta to Albania, is obviously doing something right—and has been for over a hundred years. Yet a single brand extension failure has left a scratch on the company's shining armor. Unlike Coca-Cola gum or Coca-Cola cigars, that could just be dropped and forgotten, the huge publicity attending the modern day brand extension launch, with its large—budget mass communication blitz, is a double-edged sword. Quick perceptions and early reviews can declare success or failure instantly with the headlines to drive the message home. Once a stumble is caught in the mass media a picture is created that is awfully difficult to erase.

For all its might and power and successful launches to date, it is safe to expect Coke will be under increasingly greater scrutiny as the competition and the stakes get higher.

Pepsi-Cola

One reason Coke will be under greater pressure is that Pepsi will require it. Pepsi-Cola has proved to be Coca-Cola's only serious rival over the years—hough many have tried—and has even gone so far, on occasion, to claim victory. Indeed, a 1986 book by Pepsi-Cola's then-CEO Roger Enrico was titled *The Other Guy Blinked: How Pepsi Won the Cola War*.

The victory celebration may have been a bit premature.

The "cola wars" rage on with each side bringing up fresh troops in the form of new brand extensions. Since this photo was taken, the "Pepsi generation" has witnessed the birth of Crystal Pepsi, Diet Crystal Pepsi, and Pepsi Max. (Courtesy of the Pepsi-Cola Company. Used with permission.)

First, for purposes of this example, it is important to distinguish between Pepsi-Cola beverages and its corporate parent, PepsiCo. The parent had total sales in 1981 of nearly $20 billion, compared to Coca-Cola Company's approximately $11.5 billion. In that period, however, Coke was the soft drink leader. PepsiCo's corporate position is greater largely because of its ownership of the top brands Kentucky Fried Chicken (KFC), Pizza Hut, and Taco Bell, as well as the snack foods Doritos, Fritos, and Sunchips. Coke has centered its interests in the beverage business.

Like Coca-Cola, Pepsi-Cola is the creation of a southern druggist, Caleb Bradham of North Carolina. Offering various combinations and soft drink mixtures at his drug store soda fountain, Mr. Bradham, sometime in the 1890s, developed a drink that people called Brad's drink in his honor. But by 1898 Mr. Bradham had named it Pepsi-Cola, in part because he believed the drink could also effectively settle an upset stomach (dyspepsia) and relieve the pain of peptic ulcers as well. The operation grew steadily and the Pepsi-Cola Company was formed in late 1902. With continued growth, a network of bottlers was formed, which by 1910 had burgeoned to 280 bottlers in 24 states.

While the company was tremendously successful, by 1920 fluctuations in sugar prices following the war had forced a financial reversal and a change in ownership. It also effectively forced an end to Caleb Bradham's career as a soft drink tycoon.

Reorganized and under new stewardship, the company moved to Virginia. Its new owner, however, lacked the marketing know-how to make it work and, with an extra shove from the Great Depression, Pepsi was bankrupt for the second time in 1931.

With the apparent destiny of the phoenix, the company was bought in 1931 by Charles Guth, president of a chain of confectionery stores, Loft Stores, that served an annual volume of Coca-Cola that amounted to about one percent of the beverage company's sales. Mr. Guth believed if he could switch to Pepsi without customer complaints, he could realize greater profits.

While the Pepsi-Cola Company at this time represented little more than a formula, Mr. Guth assigned Richard Ritchie, a chemist employed in his candy laboratory, to help improve that situation. Over the following two years Loft Stores bought about half of all the Pepsi syrup that was sold. What he'd hoped would be profitable turned to a loss. Coca-Cola was well-known, and Pepsi was not. In making the beverage change at the Loft Stores' fountains, sales plummeted.

Thinking the venture a complete failure by 1933, Mr. Guth attempted to sell Pepsi-Cola to Coca-Cola. Later, he made a decision that would amount to a reversal of fortune for Pepsi: to price 12-ounce bottles of Pepsi to wholesalers in such a way that retailers could offer them at the same price as the standard six or seven ounce bottles. The benefit to the customer, obviously, was that same price bought twice as much Pepsi as it did Coke. After a sputtering start, the concept was refined and by 1934, was declared a success. Pepsi appeared on its way again. Corporate politics being a fact of life, after considerable legal wrangling with Loft, Mr. Guth was forced to surrender his Pepsi stock and was out, but not before he had set it well in the direction of profitability. His belief was that the strength, popularity, and brand loyalty of Coca-Cola was so great that the only way Pepsi could make a difference was price. He was right. While Coca-Cola continued to be the clear leader in its industry, well-capitalized and even profitable during the depression, Pepsi was still that ambitious upstart company that wouldn't go away.

While the business community at-large might not have viewed Pepsi as a threat to Coke, the Coca-Cola Company was taking no chances. The David and Goliath of the soft drink industry on occasion even found themselves facing off in court . . . and not always over the predictable infringement issue.

Despite the ouster of Charles Guth as head of Pepsi, his former employer, Loft Stores, still held what had been his stock and still continued serving Pepsi in their stores. When detectives working undercover for Coca-Cola found Loft customers who ordered Coke were being served Pepsi without their knowledge, Coke sued, charging "substitution." Coke did not win its case, but went back to court, next charging Pepsi with trademark infringement. A variety of stories have circulated about exactly what happened during that period, but the end-result was a quiet out of court settlement that, in effect, dropped Coke's lawsuit and kept Pepsi going. The time was 1942.

With these early battles in the cola wars, nothing was happening that seriously threatened Coke's dominance. One area, however, where Coke still bristled was over package size. The Coca-Cola bottlers had an enormous investment in bottling equipment and materials, hence their reluctance to change from their standard 6.5-ounce bottles. This despite the fact that since 1929 they had to endure the jingle:

> Pepsi-Cola hits the spot
> Twelve full ounces, that's a lot
> Twice as much for a nickel, too
> Pepsi-Cola is the drink for you.

This classic advertising jingle, like other classics, almost never saw light. Charles Guth's successor as head of Pepsi, the entrepreneurial securities dealer Walter Mack, wanted to run the jingle only as a radio commercial, without the usual announcer's pitch. This was unheard of at the time, and both Pepsi's advertising agency and CBS' radio protested, insisting the audience wouldn't get the point of a stand-alone jingle without the normal sales message. Mr. Mack's answer to their protests was to take his message elsewhere—to radio stations who so needed the business, they were willing to allow him to do what he wanted when and how he wanted. The result was that Pepsi sales soared wherever the jingle played. CBS and the ad agency relented. Some claim this incident represented the birth of the 30-second spot, subsequently the norm in radio and television advertising.

Coca-Cola for years had relied on its slogan "the pause that refreshes," which had become an effective and recognizable tag. When Pepsi again tried to push its more-for-your-money theme with a new slogan, "more bounce to the ounce," critics were divided as to its effectiveness.

Author and former publicist Michael Gershman thought the catchy line "gave Pepsi an image boost and it became second only to Coca-Cola in soft drink sales. Pepsi sales soared and for the first time, Coca-Cola sales slumped."

Yet Harvard Professor Richard Tedlow wrote, "At the end of the 1940s, Pepsi launched yet another slogan—*more bounce to the ounce.* This slogan was designed to claim that Pepsi was not only more in volume, but in qualitative terms as well, that it had more punch and provided more energy than its competitor. The slogan commanded no credibility among consumers."

Regardless of which version one chooses to accept, Coke finally decided it needed to deal with the packaging issue and with it the matter of being considered too costly compared to Pepsi. Coke introduced king-size and family-size bottles in 1955. Alas, for taking so long to bring out its own 12-ounce bottle, Coke, the industry leader, had to suffer charges that it was copying Pepsi.

Rising production costs forced Pepsi to raise its price, thus softening its claim of being the better value for the money. Additionally, Pepsi's market share dropped as Coke's rose, and Pepsi once again believed the answer was in new leadership and new ideas. They arrived in the person of Alfred Steele, a Coca-Cola vice president, who was hired by Mr. Mack (who, while named board chairman as Mr. Steele succeeded him as president, felt he'd been treated badly and left Pepsi shortly after the changing of the guard).

The new leadership Mr. Steele provided included some 15 management people he had brought with him from Coke. Some might claim this dramatic turning point at Pepsi, allowing it to narrow the gap with its rival, came by way of hiring away the rival's key talent.

Among Mr. Steele's contributions were improving re-lationships with bottlers and "standardizing" Pepsi's taste as tested in bottling plants across the country; investing heavily in new equipment; and reducing the product's sugar content, thereby creating both a lighter-tasting drink as well as one lower in calories.

Another, and an enormously powerful aspect of the Pepsi plan focused on age. Coke had been around awhile. It was familiar, and Pepsi tried to make it look "old." The "Pepsi Generation" ad campaign was brilliant and enduring, a positioning statement of enormous impact. In its brand—building efforts, Pepsi had evolved from "Pepsi-Cola" hits the spot to "more bounce to the ounce" to "the Pepsi Generation—for those who think young."

The Pepsi Generation campaign was heavy on imagery and light on product benefits, Pepsi-Cola launched one of its most successful and long-running promotions in Dallas, Texas in 1974: The Pepsi Challenge.

Pepsi insisted that its product was preferred overwhelmingly in blind taste tests with Coke. Soon "the challenge" was expanded effectively to other markets and, in a very gutsy move, was even conducted "live" during commercial breaks on national television.

In his 1986 book *The Other Guy Blinked: How Pepsi Won the Cola Wars,* Pepsi's then CEO Roger Enrico writes "Pepsi enjoyed seventy-two straight months of market share growth. By 1974, the Pepsi-Cola brand had pulled even with Coke in food stores. In 1977, Pepsi pulled ahead—permanently."

Well ... maybe not. Claiming Pepsi won the cola wars is like asking the bully who's been pummeling you to give up. Pepsi has done well—better than well—as a Coke competitor, but in terms of soft drink sales, some six years after Mr. Enrico made that statement, Pepsi still hasn't actually *won*.

Actually, with nothing quite approaching the unfortunate experience of New Coke, Pepsi too has had its less than shining moments.

One of them was Pepsi Free.

Despite the fact that Mr. Enrico describes it as "among the most successful new brands in the history of American consumers products," this caffeine-free product *did* in fact roll out strong, before fading from sight. A caffeine-free cola with a touch of lemon flavoring just wasn't meant to be.

At the other extreme was the caffeine-*heavy* Pepsi A.M. (a product that faded so quickly, Mr. Enrico doesn't even mention it in his book). Pepsi A.M. was for people who wanted an alternative to morning coffee. Market research took note of the fact that in most regions of America, cola drinking starts around lunchtime and goes right on through the day. But in warm climates, cola is as much a welcome morning drink as coffee or tea. But what the researchers apparently didn't ask was, "If you're likely to drink a cola beverage in the morning, does it need to have A.M. on the can, or can you just drink the same cola beverage you were planning to buy later?"

Pepsi A.M. is now a collectors' item.

Diet Pepsi, on the other hand, is a smash.

While Diet Coke is far ahead, sales figures for Diet Pepsi are better than consistently respectable.

Pepsi is counting on a big future for its Crystal Pepsi clear cola—both regular and diet versions as well as the flavor extension of the line, targeted for introduction in the mid 1990s.

And if the Pepsi-Cola extension seems lacking, 1993 marked the introduction of Pepsi Max, a sugar-free cola with a sweetener the United States was slow to approve, but the rest of the world accepted. Pepsi-Cola found that the sweetner produced the closest match to the original taste.

While Roger Enrico will exploit the embarrassment of Coca-Cola over New Coke's failure (hence, his claim of Pepsi's "victory"), he adds in a sober tone "by now both of us know that neither Pepsi nor Coke wins decisively in this game. There will always be other battles on other fronts keeping us too busy to celebrate."

"And if we fail . . . well, we've both failed before and picked ourselves up off the floor."

An advertising trade magazine once asked the question "What's the big idea worth?" Will future students of advertising and marketing recognize the genius of Coca-Cola's "The pause that refreshes," or "The Real Thing," and forgive Pepsi for "You've got the right one baby—uh-huh," while appreciating "The choice of a new generation?"

Very likely, yes.

Some of Pepsi's More Memorable Slogans

Pepsi-Cola hits the spot
More bounce to the ounce
Twice as much for a penny more
Say "Pepsi, please"
Be sociable, look smart
Come alive—You're in the Pepsi
   Generation
For those who think young
The Pepsi Challenge—
   Taste that beats the others cold
You've go a lot to live . . . and Pepsi's
   got a lot to give
The choice for the new generation
You've got the right one baby—uh-huh!

It's Not So Much What's on the Inside

Dixie Cup

Over the years, many an exasperated parent has looked on as a child beams with joy upon receiving a wonderful, special gift . . . and then spends the day playing with the box in which the gift arrived. Now imagine such an occurrence in brand marketing.

Dixie Cup comes pretty close. By the 1990s Dixie Cup, a unit of the James River Corporation, had become virtually the generic name for paper cup. The brand's origin, however, begins with a statement of noble purpose of which few modern consumers are aware. Hugh Moore had an idea—one that seemed so obvious, he was sure its time had come. Early in the twentieth century, folks commonly quenched their thirst by drawing a tin dipper of water from a barrel outside of a store, railway station, or wherever. Moore looked on incredulously as people came and went, drinking from the same dipper, which was never washed and was replaced infrequently. He realized all sorts of water-borne diseases were thriving and multiplying. In this public health spirit, Moore saw a money-making opportunity. Convincing an investment banker that any number of communicable diseases might be alleviated by replacing the dippers with individual cups, the banker helped arrange a meeting with American Can Company's president, William Graham. It was Graham who put up the initial $200,000 to finance Hugh Moore's venture. Thus, in the spirit of better public health, the Public Cup Vendor Company was born in 1908 in New York City.

First, the company began producing porcelain vendor machines which, for a penny, sold a five-ounce cup of clean, cold spring water.

While most New Yorkers saw no benefit in paying for something that was readily available free, medical professionals applauded both the machine and its reason for existing. Because of this, health professionals became prime prospects to buy the machine—and they did.

As additional needs for clean, sanitary cups became more apparent, Moore realized distributing and selling cups via his vending machines made a lot more sense than trying

"serve all these hungry G. I. Joes?
sure...we use *DIXIE CUPS*

"Handing out cheer all day doesn't faze you—when you have handy helpers like paper cups.

Dixies take care of hot and cold drinks, soup, ice cream — all such things. There's no dish-

washing...and you know you're not passing along some mouth-borne infection."

Dixie Cups were intended to be sanitary, individual drinking cups, but didn't gain attention or acceptance until the company repositioned them as individual serving containers of ice cream snacks. (Dixie Cups ad courtesy of *Pages of Time*, Goodlettsville, TN. Used with permission.)

to sell water. He said, "We had to sell the ideas that drinking out of dirty glasses was dangerous."

Despite the numerous medical reports and studies available in 1908, the fact that water carried germs and germs meant disease was still treated in a somewhat cavalier manner by consumers. With a growing support from public health officers and medical practitioners, Moore was able to secure business from numerous railway companies and other businesses, but the public at large treated the sharing of public dippers and drinking cups with indifference.

Moore's Public Cup Vendor Company became the Individual Drinking Cup Company and, later, Health Kup, but as much as he believed in his product and its worthiness, its value was not readily recognized. Glasses and cups were items taken for granted. The challenge was to establish value and then identify it with a brand. Searching for a catchy, non-clinical sounding name, Moore noticed his office neighbor, the Dixie Doll Company and, from this inspiration, in 1919, Dixie Cups was born.

Still the company struggled for another four years until Moore saw an opportunity. Makers of ice cream at this time sold only in bulk, saw that their business was in a period of flat growth, and feared the simple candy bar would prove a formidable sweet shop competitor. Hugh Moore and the ice cream makers concluded they could do each other some good. After some sputtering attempts, the machinery and technology of the Dixie Cup company was employed to pack ice cream into individual two-and-a-half-ounce paper cups. The venture worked well.

Michael Gershman details the history of Dixie Cup in a book appropriately titled *Getting It Right the Second Time*. He notes that Hugh Moore and his partner Lawrence Luellen "were thrilled to be selling their cups in quantity to somebody, anybody." What neither foresaw was that by packaging ice cream in a neat, convenient container, they were also popularizing small disposable paper cups. Just as institutions later familiarized masses of people with frozen foods, consumers subconsciously began to accept the paper cup as a disposable container for solids, semi-solids, and liquids. It was not overstating the case to say that, for the first time in marketing history, a package became synonymous with the product it contained. The generic name for any kind of ice cream in any kind of handy little cup became known as a "Dixie Cup." Once the public became accustomed to the idea of the disposable paper cup, the message of how convenient and sanitary it was became just an added benefit.

In the minds of some people, Dixie Cup was first and foremost in the disposable cup business. The ice cream product became an extension of the brand. Others will contend it's the other way around—that Dixie Cup really didn't make its mark until it went into the ice cream business, thus making the disposable drinking cup the extension of the brand. In any case, Mr. Moore's original idea of a need for a safer, more sanitary product may not have initially taken the route he'd intended, but it ended up at the correct destination anyway.

In marketing terms Dixie Cup could be called an example of a product hitchhiking or piggybacking another product in order to succeed. In this case, it was hitchhiking paper cups to ice cream. It could also be termed a turn-around success, a soft product being adapted successfully for a purpose it was not originally intended. It is ironic that after succeeding at being something else, Dixie Cup has come full circle, less identified with ice cream and more commonly thought of as an individual, sanitary, disposable drinking cup.

The James River Corporation claimed at the start of the 1990s that some 42 million Dixie Cups were used each day, in various sizes and colors, for hot or cold. Some folks might consider these variations extensions on the extensions.

When a Copy Looks Better Than the Original

Xerox

Xerox achieved the type of unique brand status most brands dream about ... and their lawyers want people to know that they are none too happy about it.

The preeminent copy machine maker in the United States virtually built both the product and the market for it and, as a result, the Xerox name has been incorrectly used in reference to countless competitors' products. According to the lawyers, it's okay to ask for a copy, a photocopy, or a photostat of a document, but if you ask for "a Xerox" or "a Xerox copy" the brand of the machine used had better well *be* a Xerox or you may be opening yourself to legal action.

"Xerox" is a registered trademark of Xerox Corporation, but the word, like *Coke* and *Kleenex,* has come to be used as the generic name for its product, not just a brand. Certainly Xerox believes it stands to dilute the value of the brand name if people believe what they're getting are "Xerox" copies from machines made by Canon, Kodak, Sharp, Toshiba, or any of the numerous others.

Adding insult to injury, the company that built the market had to endure the humiliation of being outsold by "cheap imitators"—many of which were very good, incidently.

According to *Fortune,* "Even though the company brought out the first copiers in 1949, it was being clobbered in the early 1980s by Japanese rivals selling machines at the same price that it had cost Xerox to make them. Xerox's biggest corporate sin: arrogantly taking customers for

Xerox may be the world's best-known office copy machine, but it took diversification into the financial services industry to save the company from disaster. This ad for Xerox Life shows one example of how they did it. (Ad used with permission and courtesy of Xerox Life.)

granted. The company wasn't too effective with employees either."

"I frankly thought Xerox was on its way out of business," recalls former Xerox CEO David Kearns.

Once Japanese-made products had been dismissed by the United States and other countries as cheap and inferior. Brands like Sony, Toyota, Yamaha, and Nissan changed that. Modern Japanese technology and competitiveness—especially in the electronics and automotive industries—frequently produced products that set new standards for quality.

Japan's entry into the copy machine field was no less impressive.

To keep matters in order, as well as in perspective, it must be acknowledged that Xerox is an absolutely first-class company. Its history is the stuff of which folklore is made: In the 1930s, Chester Carlson, living in a cramped one-room apartment, working in a makeshift laboratory in Astoria, Queens, New York, invents a process called xerography—document copying without printing or tracing. He tries to sell this process to virtually every important company in the office equipment business, including IBM, General Electric, RCA, Remington Rand, and about 20 others. They all pass. Finally, a relatively small operation in Rochester, New York, The Haloid Company, shows an interest in Carlson and his process. After a shaky start, in its crudest form, the process that would in effect revolutionize print communications was unerway.

In 1955 Carlson signed over full title to all of his patents in exchange for 50,000 shares of Haloid stock. The process was generating sufficient interest that the company had changed its name to Haloid Xerox. (By 1961 it had evolved into "The Xerox Corporation.")

The company, despite numerous fits and starts, grew rapidly. On occasion, the company would delay introduction of new models for fear of smothering sales of existing models that were still selling well. The "Xerox machine" was the essential piece of office equipment after the telephone. It made even the smallest company look big.

By the 1960s, Xerox profits were high, sales were great, and the company had indeed achieved the status of "household word." Yet, some managers occasionally wondered what would happen to Xerox if someone else came up with a cheaper or faster product than its now fully perfected process of xerography.

It is ironic that Chester Carlson had taken his early idea to office equipment/computer giant IBM and been turned away. In later years talks were initiated more than once between the two companies for the purpose of selling patents or entering into joint ventures, but nothing ever came of them. By 1970, IBM wanted in, but their position in the market—at least for the copy machine segment—was to be an afterthought. As Al Ries and Jack Trout note in their 1981 book *Positioning*, "IBM is a much bigger company than Xerox and has awesome resources of technology, work force and money. Yet what happened when IBM introduced a line of copiers competitive with those of Xerox?

"Not much. Xerox still has a share of the copier market several times that of IBM."

Their point is that the first one to succeed in a given industry or category and become the market leader has the advantage of being so identified as to "own" that market. Even so powerful and formidable a competitor as IBM could not shake the fact from people's minds that a copy machine was a *Xerox* machine.

Xerox had built a brand with so much perceived equity, it could beat back the strongest potential competition. Then, in the parlance of the business community, the wheel fell off.

Mainly, two factors kicked in—either of which might have been enough to do in the company. One problem was external, the other internal. In the 1992 book *Prophets in the Dark,* former Xerox CEO David Kearns describes the internal situation, noting that "Given the environment (of our success) it was easy for managers to get a little arrogant and stop paying attention to what the competition we did have was doing and to drift out of intimate contact with the customer. We got into big trouble mostly because we stopped listening to the customer. Sooner or later, that sort of deafness can be fatal.

"There was also no real quality control to speak of in the company, no all-pervasive attitude that the products must be as good as humanly possible. Quality in those days was considered nothing more than an expense—and who wanted extra expenses?"

Kearns points out that even Xerox pricing policies were alienating their customers, and one could hardly blame them for being upset. Their pricing was "about the most bewildering strategy I ever came across; you'd get dizzy looking at all the presentations."

At the same time, the external situation grew more threatening. While managers at Xerox had expected at some point that Japanese companies would enter their business, no one paid much attention to the threat. Presumably the sentiment was that if Xerox was strong enough and smart enough to outgrow giants like IBM and Kodak, it could handle a foreign challenger. Further, no one took note of two points characteristic of fine Japanese companies: they offered a high level of quality for products manufactured at a very low level of cost.

Savin, in a joint venture with Japanese manufacturer Ricoh, offered a copier that broke down less often, was easier to repair, and was priced at less than half the cost of a comparable Xerox machine. Obviously, it was a huge success.

And it was only the beginning.

Other Japanese companies kept the pressure on and chipped away at Xerox market share. Much of the chipping seemed to be in very large chunks as the perception became reality that while Xerox was still the original and the U.S. leader in the field, as copiers went, there were fine—even superior—machines available at lower cost.

At the same time, a Xerox attempt at diversification into the non-copier field was not going well. IBM tried its hand at getting into Xerox's business and stumbled. In an ironic turn, Xerox's foray into the computer-based information systems business was a similar failure.

Xerox had purchased a company called Scientific Data Systems and, treating it as a brand extension of the copier, of sorts, renamed it Xerox Data Systems. The billion-dollar acquisition depended heavily on government contracts—particularly for the space program—for its survival. The acquisition occurred roughly at a time when such contracts were drying up, and the venture was a money-loser virtually from day one. With Xerox's stock price falling, the company tried a number of reconfigurations of Xerox Data Systems, separating operating units, and separating functions. Finally, after six years and enormous losses, Xerox folded XDS.

Yet the company pursued other ventures into the personal computer area, seeing it quite rightly as an emerging growth area. Alas, it was not in the cards for Xerox to participate profitably in this emergence. With all the quality, cost-effective alternatives, Xerox remained, in everyone's eyes, a copy machine company—and one that was being beaten up by the Japanese copier companies at that. One reason is, again, Xerox's failure to listen to its customers, to take the pulse of the market. Virtually all Xerox copy machines were leased by customers, who then bought copier supplies and maintenance from the company. By the 1970s this all changed as the competition had made ownership very affordable. Leases were not renewed. Contracts were cancelled. David Kearns examined the totality of the situation and announced "The deeper we studied what was going on in our industry, the worse things looked."

The only possible way out of the quagmire, the company concluded, lay in two options: diversify and virtually change the entire way Xerox did business, from manufacturing and quality control to pricing and marketing. Amidst much debate, the company decided to do both.

Diversification took the form of acquiring companies that were (1) more tied to the service industry than to manufacturing and (2) looking at industries where past Xerox problems were unlikely to reoccur. To put it bluntly, that meant looking for companies in which a competitor, such as Japanese industries, could not likely move in and do better for less cost.

Starting in 1982 with the purchase of the very prosperous casualty insurance company operation, Crum & Forster, Xerox Financial Services was born. Two profitable investment banking businesses were acquired: Van Kampen Merritt and Furman Selz. Xerox Life and Xerox Credit were added, and a stake in VMS Realty Partners rounded out the mix. Ultimately, the rough economy, radical changes affecting the insurance industry, and the tax law changes that virtually wiped out real estate syndication caused at least a couple of these units to crash and burn. But through most of the 1980s Xerox Financial Services was exactly the right prescription to offset the losses on the parent company's office products side and to contribute mightily to the Xerox bottom line.

The major change, important for both its revolutionary makeover of Xerox and its long-term importance, was in the manufacturing, pricing, and marketing processes. The emphasis was on quality and, in a marked departure from the past, on listening to customers.

What David Kearns described in his book about his Xerox years as "the blooming of quality" had corporate problem-solvers organize problem areas into six principles on which their 1990s "intensification efforts for quality" would be based:

1. A customer defines our business.

2. Our success depends upon the involvement and empowerment of trained and highly motivated people.

3. Line management must lead quality improvement.

4. Management develops, articulates, and deploys clear direction and objectives.

5. Quality challenges are met and satisfied.

6. The business is managed and improved by using facts.

Product quality improved. Reliability improved. Customer satisfaction increased. Labor overhead was trimmed by 50 percent; materials overhead was cut by 40 percent. The process of relationship building went into high gear.

Xerox's efforts had not only reversed the company's slide, they rocketed Xerox back to respectability as a leading world-wide manufacturer. In 1982 Xerox didn't have a single machine rated best-in-its-class by analysts. By 1992

Xerox models were ranked the leading machines in all seven copier categories.

But perhaps most significant was the fact that Xerox was the first major American company targeted by the Japanese to turn the tide and regain market share solely by their own efforts—without government assistance or legislation.

Xerox came back, but without question, it did it the hard way. Perhaps the key point that saved the company was, ultimately, its management's willingness to take a hard, critical—and honest—look at itself, and to react. Corporate arrogance had hurt it badly, and that had to be changed. The company needed to listen to its customers and to be responsive. It needed to emphasize quality and price competitiveness. It wasn't enough just to be Xerox.

It needed, too, to look at those acquisitions and divisions to which it had attached its name. The failure of Scientific Data Systems was compounded by the fact that the company at the time of its liquidation was called Xerox Data Systems. The ultimate collapse of Crum & Forster would have had far worse implications had it been called Xerox Property & Casualty Company. Diversification, brand extension, and acquisitions are legitimate options when they make sense financially and enhance the core brand or company's image—but do not expose the company to any great degree of damage if the extension or acquisition fails.

Xerox clearly did some things very right and very wrong, and even their top brass concede that for a long time survival—much less profit—was hardly a foregone conclusion. Most would likely agree that the turnaround could have been effected sooner and at a lower cost, but egos obscured the company's view of its problems. Perhaps Xerox was counting on its fictional advertising character, the lovable Brother Dominick, to ask for Divine intervention. In the final analysis, they were smart not to wait.

. . . And Now for Something Extra

Wrigley Extra

In 1990, the Wm. Wrigley Jr. Company maintained a 48 percent market share, of the $1.3 billion U.S. gum market, more than double that of its nearest competitor.

"We make two things," a Wrigley executive remarked, "chewing gum and money for our stockholders."

That wasn't always the case.

Around 1891, William Wrigley started a chewing gum company while running a baking powder company. A tireless promoter, Wrigley planned to use the gum as a giveaway to those who bought his baking powder.

He first marketed a brand called Vassar gum to women, adding Juicy Fruit and Wrigley's Spearmint gum in 1893. Times were tough, and it was a shaky beginning for the company financially.

William Wrigley had long been regarded as a salesman, a showman, and a marketing genius. He reportedly attributed his ultimate success in business to a lack of fear, saying "I've been broke three times since I started in business and it didn't cause me a minute's loss of sleep." At the time of his death in 1931, two years after the stock market crash, Wrigley left an estate worth some $20 million.

He was a risk taker who borrowed heavily, advertised mightily and believed hard in his ideas. He also believed in marketing very, very aggressively.

The company's philosophy a century later is somewhat more conservative, but still aggressive. Already leading the field with its Spearmint, Doublemint, Juicy Fruit, and Big Red chewing gums, the company chose to pass up the candy and mint segments of the confectionery market, though some thought such an extension logical. Perhaps Wrigley recalled the attempt by Life Savers to expand the tremendous popularity of Life Savers candy into Life Savers gum, a costly and embarrassing failure. Another attempt at extension, Gummy Life Savers, stumbled in test markets.

The Wrigley marketing philosophy was customer driven. The company saw as its mission to "sell the customers what they want to buy, when they want to buy it, where they want to buy it."

With their core brands stable and highly profitable, the Wrigley marketers looked to the fast-growing sugar-free segment of the chewing gum market where the American Chicle Group Division of Warner-Lambert was racking up healthy sales with its very successful Trident brand. Wrigley's sugar-free gum, Orbit, rolled out strong and was building fast when a negative health story said an ingredient in Orbit could be hazardous to health. Sales for the fledgling brand collapsed in the United States, though elsewhere in the world, the product continues to sell.

Wrigley executives insist that just getting a product out for the sake of being represented in the category is not their style. Wrigley Group Vice President for Marketing, Ronald O. Cox maintains, "We are probably more judicious than many companies when it comes to line extension. What we try to do is focus on what would be a good product to offer, rather than just react to trends."

Cox adds, "We're also very sensitive in certain areas. First there's the confusion on the part of consumers with so much product out there and secondly, the trade has to figure out how they're going to stock 12,000 variations of a single product."

Line extensions and brand extensions are not new to Wrigley. The company has done well with them, relying heavily on market research and thinking long term. "We respond to what's important to the consumer, not to reports of 'what's hot,'" notes Ron Cox. Aware that the 1980s was a time of instant successes, instant failures, and instant gratification, Wrigley maintained a policy that disregarded pressure to rush to market with products they didn't believe in.

According to Wrigley marketing executives, line extensions should be designed to broaden the appeal of the line to consumers. Line extensions also create a danger of cannibalization of the brand. A short-term management approach normally gets in the way of long-term considerations, executives believe. For example, short-term management ignores the volume of the product in the current year's pipeline, takes a "worry about it next year" attitude, and focuses concern on the potential of the competition to gain an advantage.

The long-term approach is, to Wrigley, the more viable way to meet consumer needs and prevent switching to competitive brands due to "voids" in the assortment of products offered. The key, they believe, is not to get too greedy and to allow enough time to provide the highest level of quality to extensions of the product line.

Cox refers to brand extension as the "buzzword of the '80s," an opinion shared by a number of seasoned marketers. The belief is that one can save advertising and marketing costs by extending a well-known name into new fields. Certainly there are numerous examples on both sides as to whether or not it works, but what is the criteria for determining success? Is it sales? Market share? Profits? And under a long-term strategy, what time frame affords a reasonable period of determination?

Wrigley executives believe successful brand extension depends more on the "art" of marketing than on science. They believe, too, that the best approach is based on five considerations:

1. Product quality has to be a competitive plus.

2. Extension areas must be chosen carefully.

3. "Up front logic" doesn't always work.

4. Brand extensions can't be viewed as "marketing cost-saving efforts."

5. Beware of design firms selling brand extension "scams"—that is, putting the brand name and logo on a product that no experience or research tells you is likely to succeed.

This approach appears to have worked well for Wrigley. While the success of competitor Trident may have contributed to the timing of their introduction of Orbit—and later Wrigley's Extra—market research was already steering the company in that direction. Wrigley's Extra grew from a five-percent market share to forty percent of the sugar-free chewing gum segment in seven years. But the bigger story than just the line introduction of sugar-free chewing gum, may well be the introduction of a new flavor, Winterfresh. With the line already boasting the traditional favorite flavors (spearmint, peppermint, and cinnamon), new Winterfresh was touted as a breath freshener as well as a chewing gum.

One report had nervous marketers pitching the idea to Wrigley, pointing out there was previously no such flavor as winterfresh among chewing gums, mints, or candies and that this could be a risky introduction. Wrigley's response was to remind his people that there was also no such flavor as "doublemint" until they invented it, named it, and made it a success.

Winterfresh Wrigley's Extra was not only a huge and early success, but, as a trademarked Wrigley property, would be a new extension to the company's Freedent line of chewing gum (the highly successful line that offers the benefit to consumers of not sticking to dentures).

Advertising Age has noted that "sugared gums got a sales boost (in 1991) from the twenty-five cent five-stick packs and the ten-unit multi-packs. The Wrigley company credits that 'value-pricing' with producing the U.S. volume increase ... "

Part of Wrigley's strategy has long been to grow the market for chewing gum, not just to serve the markets that existed. In the words of one Wrigley executive, speaking of the multi-pack "if a consumer has one pack of gum in his or her pocket or purse, he or she will consume that pack of gum. But if we can get more sticks and more packs into the pocket or purse, the result will be more chewing gum consumed." Promoting increased chewing was addressed in an ad campaign that urged smokers to chew (more) gum as they find themselves in designated non-smoking buildings and areas. The campaign's theme was that Wrigley Spearmint gum is the smoker's alternative.

While persons attempting to stop smoking have been encouraged for years to chew gum, this campaign took the approach of saying, Don't wait until you've quit ... start chewing and enjoying the gum now.

Despite ad spending being down a bit and sales figures being up a bit, it would seem Wrigley's Freedent, Wrigley's Extra, and "the smoker's alternative" campaign, as well as promotion of core brands, has put the company's estimated $125 million annual advertising budget to good use. Aggressive and conservative, they've come a long way from the days of "the Doublemint Twins" and a message that invited consumers to "chew your little troubles away."

While limiting extension of its core brands to various package sizes, Wrigley's gave the full line extension treatment to its Freedent and enormously successful Extra sugarfree gum with packaging, flavors, and the creation of a new taste in "Winter Fresh." (Courtesy of the Wm. Wrigley Jr. Company. Used with permission.)

CREATING, MANAGING, AND MARKETING BRAND EQUITY

Chapter Six

A Crash Course in Brand Marketing

*"If you have something of importance
to say, for God's sake start at the end."*

—Sarah Jeannette Duncan

In the film, *Nothing in Common,* a successful, yuppie advertising executive is about to drive his father to the hospital in
a new Jeep. His father looks upon the vehicle with some
disdain, at its lack of style and status. He mutters "When are
you going to get a real car?"

His son immediately fires back "This is a real car. *I look
good in this car."*

There you have it—the essence of the results of advertising and marketing. He *looked good* in the car.

What he meant, of course, was that he *felt* good in the
car because it represented an image he wanted to step into
and wrap around himself: the yuppie in his jeep—hip,
young, clever, and out of the mainstream.

The right car.
The right watch.
The right wine.

One does not wrap himself or herself in an image adopted, or to which one aspires, defined by generics. Brands reflect an image—a personality. Brands help define what's *right* in products. The marketer who tries to build a brand on price alone may get a sale (or several sales), but will most likely lose the customer to the next brand that advertises a lower price.

Brand loyalty is built on quality, price, image, and service—elements that constitute value.

Brand equity is the value in and of a brand.

To create, manage and market brand equity, you must do the following:

1. *Use research.* Know all that you can about the pluses and minuses of your own product or service and those of your competitors—past, current, and potential. Know what your customers want and how much they are willing to pay for it. Know to what degree service and quality are a consideration. Remember that most every one says they *want* service and quality, but will they—can they—pay for it? Research can minimze the potential for costly mistakes. Use research to learn what your customers like and dislike. Tuning out customer feedback can be fatal to a business.

2. *Use your marketing plan.* Too often marketing plans are developed to impress a CEO or a board of directors. They are presented and accepted, then languish in a file drawer. Marketing success is not dumb luck. A marketing plan should be like a map, carefully drawn, showing how to get from one place to another with shortcuts included. Your plan should include a situation analysis, objective, strategy and tactics, budget, and a timeline with

benchmarks to evaluate success or the need to modify the plan.

3. *Define the core brand's position clearly.* Remember the old commercial that began with the couple arguing about whether Certs was a candy or a breath mint? Don't let someone else position your product. What is it? Who is it for? What are its strengths and weaknesses—alone and relative to competition? What is your product or your company's reputation?

4. *Qualify your plan.* Who are your customers (men, women, teens, seniors, ethnics, generations)? Does your core product meet the needs of one or all market segments? Should you consider a brand extension to meet the needs and/or desires of a particular market segment? Will doing so—or not doing so—cost you market share, or will it cannibalize the market for the core product?

5. *Define the value of your core product.* Value is price, quality, and image. Is your product price competitive with that of the other brands? If higher, is the value clear enough to justify the extra cost? If lower, does that "cheapen" the perceived value of your product? What is the perception of your level of quality, alone and relative to competition? Is your image well-defined? Consider the impression that was left by such lines as "For those who think young," "I'd rather fight than switch," "We bring good things to life," "Nature's most perfect food, " "The Real Thing," "You deserve a break today," and "Where America shops." The product without a defined image suggests its appeal is to no one in particular.

6. *Consider brand extension as adding value.* A good product, doing well, should be supported, not tampered with. But when the pulse of the market creates a need or desire, consider a companion with its own defined value—sugar free, sodium free, low cholesterol, no additives, biodegradable, recyclable, etc.

7. *Have a reason for a brand extension.* Often a brand extension is a "competitive counterpunch." Let your research tell you there is a need and/or desire for the brand extension. Bringing something out because a competitor did is risky and expensive.

8. *Define primary and secondary goals.* A primary goal usually is (or should be) generating sales or revenue. Is your product's goal market dominance? For the benefit of a social cause? Be clear about if and how goals of your core product and brand extension may be the same (competing) or complementing each other.

9. *Don't neglect public relations.* PR is often dismissed as a perfunctory process of sending out news releases that announce promotions of people or events basically just trying to get a little press. Newsletters, hotlines, surveys, studies, event sponsorships, educational grants, subsidies of the arts, educational texts/audios/videos, and guest columns or editorials can help define the personality of a company or brand. Consider the impact of the General Electric 24-hour service hotline, the Citibank 24-hour Citiphone, the Mobil Oil grant to Masterpiece Theater, sponsorship of the U.S. Olympic Team—these are all the public relations programs that influence consumers and regula-

tors, positioning the brand name as a good corporate citizen of the community and someone nice to do business with. Don't underestimate the value of good publicity.

10. *Advertise.* Yes, it can be expensive, but if done right, advertising is much more of an investment than an expense. To control the space, what is said, where it's said, and how often can have a powerful influence on the impression left behind. It is essential to successful brand building. There is a reason that the largest, most successful companies in the world are the largest advertisers: it works. TV networks now even run specials about the best TV commercials ever made—and audiences sit through 60 to 90 minutes of classic commercials (separated by current paid commercials). Where would some of our best brands be without their ads: The Marlboro Man, Pepsi—the choice of a new generation, "Just for the taste of it—Diet Coke!" "Where's the beef?" "A Kodak Moment," "The Heartbeat of America?" When a brand takes its ad campaign seriously (even the funny ones), it creates attention, recognition, awareness, loyalty, and image. Advertising works. Consider how many brands' market share plummeted when they reduced or eliminated advertising.

11. *Recognize that promotions are tricky.* They should be used to create recognition and to help build brand loyalty, not just for "trial" or discounting. Sweepstakes can serve to help build a database, but tend to shift attention from the product to the trip to Hawaii or Disneyland or whatever prizes are offered. Try to make the promotion relate to the product, such as AT&T or MCI offering members

of the military free phone calls to family members on Sunday or a major oil company running an energy-saver promotion or Betty Crocker or Campbell Soup sponsoring a recipe contest. The legal restrictions on contests and promotions have caused as much as 20 percent of the contest ad space to be devoted to detailing restrictions and disclaimers. The result is that too often the participants are interested only in the promotion, not in the advertiser's product, and that certainly doesn't add up to a successful program for the advertisers. Good promotions such as the frequent-flyer or frequent diner points that award discounts and rebates on a product are the most sensible and effective.

12. *Remember the USP (Unique Selling Proposition).* This basic rule of advertising is often overlooked in favor of glitz or dazzle. The USP is to give the customer both a reason to buy and to distinguish your brand from the competitions'. Your core brand should have a unique selling proposition, and your brand extension should have *its own* unique selling proposition, not just exist because there's a core product.

13. *Don't expand your line just to look bigger.* No, bigger isn't always better. There are limits to shelf, storage, and display space. There is also confusion among consumers about the proliferation of products. Competition is a healthy thing, but there are limits to what people will accept. The existence of hundreds of brands of cigarettes is difficult to justify. How "unique" can they be from one another after a point? Focus on creating and managing the equity of your brand, and let your extensions be

logical, market-wise extensions, not product explosions.

14. *Be honest and ethical.* When a company invests talent, energy, and resources in creating value for its brand name, it is just good business sense to protect its integrity. Lawsuits and corporate crises can tarnish a brand's name (often unfairly), but an open, candid (and swift) response can maintain and restore trust. American Express, one of the best names in the business, is the subject of at least a few devastating, but well-documented, books that reveal a heavy-handed, unethical underside that could only be addressed by the CEO resigning. Sears Roebuck & Company's property manipulations, store closings, and layoffs and major market miscalculations left an image suggesting a management out of touch—and not caring very much about it. The Exxon Valdez tanker oil spill is a classic case of arrogance and as a response to inept action. These are only a few giant companies that could have turned their troubles into potential opportunities to do well by doing good. A pattern of public honesty and ethical corporate behavior creates a reservoir of goodwill from which a company can draw in times of crisis. Trump, Milken, Helmsley . . . these are a few of the big names of the 1980s who alienated so many people that when they ran into trouble, masses cheered their falling from favor. Don't exceed credibility in what you promise. That's only good business. Projecting a positive image costs no more than projecting a negative one.

15. *Be careful with attack ads and comparisons.* This was a "bold" idea of the 1980s, but its time has passed.

Most ads that attack a competitor's product have tended to backfire by giving the competitor attention, interest, and perhaps even sympathy. The best advertising emphasizes the benefits of the product advertised. If the best you can say about your product is that your competitor's product is bad, you don't have much going for your product. Take the high road. Be positive.

16. *Include a promise with your product.* Whether your core product or your brand extension, give people a reason to buy your product. Stress the benefits. Add value. Remove real or potential irritants. Create a climate of acceptance.

17. *If you can, be first. If you can't be first, be better.* This is a pretty self-explanatory point. The market rewards imagination and innovation. Being original gets noticed. Being first earns pioneer status and gives you the advantage of being the probable market leader. But if you can't be first, be better. The market doesn't need another cola or cigarette or toothpaste with baking soda just to have them. Make your product stand for something. Remember the USP, whether you're first out of the gate or last.

18. *Listen.* David Kearns, the former CEO of Xerox Corporation said the company ran into big problems when it stopped listening to its customers. Al Ries and Jack Trout offer "success often leads to arrogance and arrogance to failure." In an earlier volume, I shared a particular favorite observation: there are those who listen and those who simply wait to talk. Bless the listeners. You can learn a lot by observing and being receptive to comments and

suggestions. Sure, in all likelihood, you'll hear a lot of stupid, irrelevant things, but if just a little comes your way that's worth hearing—be it favorable or critical—the intelligent marketer or administrator recognizes its worth.

Chapter Seven

The Future of Brand Marketing

Today and Tomorrow ...

Consumers care about the workings of business more than
ever before. Not so long ago, few people would have chosen
to patronize—or stay away from—a Pizza Hut or Taco Bell
restaurant merely because they are owned by Pepsi. It was
of little concern to a hungry traveller that Pillsbury owned
and operated Burger King. That's changed now. Some folks,
firmly committed to the "buy American" philosophy not
only won't buy German or Japanese cars or stereo equipment, but will bypass even a Burger King *and* a bag of
Pillsbury flour *and* getting their eyeglasses from Pearle Vision center because all of these companies are owned by
London's Grand Metropolitan. Large multi-national con-
glomerates are not new, but people's attitude towards
them—and the people who support them—can change with
the latest issue of *Fortune* or *Business Week*.

Business news used to be only of interest to business
people. But consider that the story of the takeover of RJR
Nabisco was not only a number one national best-seller for

months, but became major motion picture, *Barbarians at the Gate.*

Oliver Stone's *Wall Street* was named best picture of the year at the same time *People* magazine was featuring Donald Trump, Rupert Murdock, and Michael Milken in its pages. Those stodgy investment bankers and corporate moguls of old were major national celebrities, listed in TV features and gossip columns along with rock stars.

With such high profile corporate posturing comes an upside: a broader audience and greater visibility and awareness of a company and a product. The downside, of course, is that similar mass audiences get to learn immediately about—and react to—boycotts, news of falling profits, product liability suits, and "green mail."

When Nestlé was the target of a worldwide boycott stemming from its marketing of infant formula to third world countries, the nightly news told of the boycott and its effect on Nestlé units from its candy bars to Stouffer frozen dinners—and Stouffer Hotels.

Global instant communication is more than championship prizefights, rock concerts, and war coverage coming into millions of people's homes; it's also news of drug company suits, oil company price hikes, and automobiles that explode on impact. If there were ever such a thing as managed news or "spin control," influencing how a negative story might be interpreted positively, it's over. Marketers into the twenty-first century must not only understand this, but learn to use and even exploit it.

In an earlier book called *Getting the Best from Your Ad Agency*, I predicted ad clutter would continue to annoy consumers, merchandising would become a more important part of the marketing mix, research would get less of the budget, and cable TV would be responsible for a lot of the changes in the way marketers market and the way customers respond. As this volume goes to press, remember that offering predictions can be risky, but I've yet to be embarrassed by my earlier crystal ball gazing.

Ad clutter continues to make it harder for an advertiser's message to be noticed and harder still for it to be believed in the myriad of sincerely represented claims with little or no credibility. The "tune-out" factor is high. Columnist George Lazarus calls this "marketing immunity." The Pulitzer Prize-winning humor writer Dave Barry has pointed out to his millions of readers, "We have learned to accept that, even though these people have gone to the trouble and expense of buying the advertisements in which they claim they are in the business of fixing things, many of them will not show up . . . I'll tell you what American businesses do a good job of: pretending they care about customers."

Ouch!

Barry's remarks find considerable empathy with consumers who realize testimonials and endorsements in ads are paid for. The customer satisfaction picture is pretty bleak. A *Time* cover story in the mid-1980s asked the question "Why is service so bad?" As yet, no one seems to have come up with a good answer, but that hasn't stopped many companies from continuing to suggest that *their* clients are happy, so we must be talking about someone else. Alas, clutter and lack of credibility go hand in hand. Marketers in the future must again, if they can't reduce the clutter, stress the benefits of the product or service to the consumer, the *USP*. And don't exceed credibility. People will actually try a product because it has a benefit to them, even if it's not the eighth wonder of the world.

On the research front, Joe Klein writing in *Newsweek* in March 1993, noted, "for the past quarter century, American business has been great at R(esearch), but too impatient to be very good at D(evelopment). It's been left to the Japanese, and others, to take American ideas—like VCRs—and figure out how to manufacture them."

Another problem has been the reluctance of too many companies to invest in research, believing it would only tell them things they already know. Hence, like ad budgets, research has been slashed. Unfortunately, it's the corporate arrogance that hasn't been reduced to a level where common sense can prevail. Research tells you what you need to know about your product, company, competition, strengths, and weakness in the marketplace. Advertising presents your image and your message in the best possible terms, the greatest number of times, to the people who need to see it. A reluctance to invest in these key areas, a cautious approach lacking in imagination, seems to be guiding the businesses of the 1990s. There was never a better opportunity to remember that some highly successful ventures were launched in what many described as "the worst possible time." Success has always grown from commitment.

And on the cable TV front? With long-range plans getting shorter and the promise of 500 channels (keep that remote control ready), TV will be more like magazines, with a dedicated channel for the most narrow, specific, and esoteric tastes (science, nature, history, comedy, art, cooking, weather, foreign languages, medicine, law, and much more).

Gone is the dominance of the television networks that programmed for the masses. The emphasis will be on niches, presenting a highly targeted avenue to brand marketers.

Sports Illustrated, a perennial favorite that has been "must" reading for sports fans for years, has joined the tech generation with a series of sports videos. The company has also introduced *Sports Illustrated for Kids* to market to younger readers today and prepare them to become the *Sports Illustrated* readers of tomorrow. *Money* magazine has done the same thing. *Money for Kids* teaches youngsters about saving and investing and getting ready to read *Money* when they grow up. Both magazine ideas came from the marketing minds of Time Warner, the parent company, no stranger to brand extension and promotions.

The jury is still out on movie theater advertising. Initially, audiences resented having to sit in a theater and watch commercials after having paid their admission fee. But as some of the spots from Coca-Cola, American Express and a few others proved to be very entertaining, resentment receded. This approach can only work in the future if (1) clutter is held to a minimum, (2) the spots are uniquely entertaining and suited to the big screen, and (3) they are not the same as TV commercials that have already had small screen exposure. Some movie studios have already put into the theater/exhibitor's rental agreement that no commercials will be shown with their film.

The rising cost of health care and medications has spurred increased interest in generic drugs. Pharmaceutical companies, in a move to counter this trend, have run ads in major weekly news magazines, similar to those normally run in trade papers, encouraging consumers to become familiar with specific drug brand names. These ads, four-color, high gloss, and with information normally only provided to a doctor, are designed to encourage patients to ask their doctors to consider treating them with a specific drug—by name:

➧ The ad for the nicotine patch Habitrol carries the pre-headline "No one believed I would ever really quit smoking." A testimonial then follows.

➧ Another bold, colorful ad in the same magazine carried the same pitch, but for Nicotrol.

➧ Still another patch, Nicoderm, told the same story in the same media.

➠ The national news magazine four-color ads for Card-izem CD invite the patient to "ask your doctor if Cardizem CD is right for you" and to call for a free quarterly newsletter on healthy living.

➠ Norplant System has run color spreads in national newsweeklies selling consumers on Levonorgestrel implants as a birth control method.

Sending a message to Congress, as well as the public, the Pharmaceutical Manufacturers Association placed ads in newsweeklies with headlines like "Ask Mike what he'd do if you took away the ulcer drug that's saving him from a $25,000 operation." The pharmaceutical companies are well aware that the public perceives them as "drug" companies reaping huge profits while others suffer hard times. These ads are to warm up and personalize the companies' relationship with the patients and regulators. It is, in effect, lobbying through the print media, while building a brand name.

An idea that marketers have been trying to sell for years is the interactive one. Phone companies and retailers have joined together in the past with banks and utilities. Home shopping networks brought the concept a bit of show biz sizzle. Inevitably, one day, most everything a consumer could want could be viewed, ordered, and paid for by a techno-hybrid of TV/phone/computers. Cocooning will look more like hibernation, as people never leave home.

No discussion of the future of brands should overlook the earth. That is to say, the public has a greater concern than ever before about buying and using products that are both safe and good for the environment. These "green" products carry labels attesting to their safety and purity. One tendency among purists is to go into overkill with "all natural" products that cost more. Historically, fashions run in cycles: small cars are out/in/out again; styrofoam is in/out/okay again; green, clear, and other all-natural products are in/expensive/overrated/in again. Being good for our environment is always good, it's the trendy aspect of it that comes and goes and the marketer has to know the public's tolerance levels. Once again, a product should be what it is based on quality and marketed for its benefits, not its trendiness.

Since the concept of selling itself came into being, it's safe to assume trust was a factor in how people decided who they'd do business with. Thus, the idea of "brand" names was born. And a trusted brand name on a new product borrows against established trust to get a trial and evaluation. As trends come and go, the trusted names survive.

In April 1993, *The Wall Street Journal* wrote, "Is brand loyalty dead?" Nearly, say a crowd of stock investors.

Brand loyalty dead?

Hardly, although it may be napping.

Simply put, business—and even its trends—run in cycles. In a tough economy, interest rises in generic brands . . . only to be replaced by a return of desire for quality and image: a brand name.

Private labels—house brands—are on the rise. But as manufacturers add words like "special," "premium," "gourmet," or "limited" and charge prices comparable to name brands, ultimately the name brand will win out. Rarely do private label products enjoy a comparable level of promotion to brand names, so they rarely enjoy the same level of loyalty that comes from familiarity with a name.

Brands will be around as long as the marketers of the brands keep their fingers on the pulse of the marketplace. And that pulse can quicken rapidly. Be ready . . . and good luck.

BIBLIOGRAPHY

"100 Leading National Advertisers." *Advertising Age,* September 23, 1992.

Alsop, Ronald and Bill Abrams, eds. 1986. *The Wall Street Journal on Marketing.* New York: Dow Jones & Company.

Barry, Dave. 1992. *Dave Barry Does Japan.* New York: Random House.

Boyd, Harper W. Jr. and Robert M. Clewett. 1962. *Contemporary American Marketing.* Homewood, Ill.: Richard D. Irwin Publishers.

Cappo, Joe. 1990. *FutureScope: Success Strategies for the 1990s and Beyond.* Chicago: Longman.

Clark, Eric. 1988. *The Want Makers.* New York: Viking Press.

"Coke II Spot Goes Flat on Persuasion." *Advertising Age,* September 7, 1992.

Cote, Kenneth. "David Kearns: How I Saved the Titanic." *Fortune,* January,1992.

Donaton, Scott. "Playboy Expands to Custom Titles." *Advertising Age,* May 18, 1992.

Enrico, Roger and Jesse Korbluth. 1986. *The Other Guy Blinked*. New York: Bantam Books.

Fahey, Alison. "Coke II Sneaks into Cola Combat Zone." *Advertising Age*, May 11, 1992.

Gershman, Michael. 1990. *Getting It Right the Second Time*. San Francisco: Addison-Wesley Publishing.

Hambleton, Ronald. 1987. *The Branding of America*. New York: Yankee Books.

Harris, Thomas L. 1991. *The Marketer's Guide to Public Relations*. New York: John Wiley & Sons.

Harvey, Richard D. "Why Cola Growth is Stalling in Food Stores." *Advertising Age*, June 22, 1992.

Hisrich, Robert D. 1990. *Marketing*. New York: Barron's.

Hwang, Suien L. "RJR Sees Its Cigarette Sales Recovering." *The Wall Street Journal*, May 14, 1992.

Jones, John Philip. 1986. *What's in a Name? Advertising and the Concept of Brands*. New York: Lexington Books.

Kearns, David T. and David A. Nadler. 1992. *Prophets in the Dark*. New York: Harper Business.

Klein, Joe. "Clinton's Project Addiction." *Newsweek*, March 22, 1993.

Lazarus, George and Bruce Wexler. 1988. *Marketing Immunity: Breaking Through Customer Resistance*. Homewood, Ill.: Dow Jones Irwin.

Liesse, Julie. "Brand Extensions Take Center Stage." *Advertising Age*, March 8, 1993.

Liesse, Julie. "Brands in Trouble." *Advertising Age*, December 2, 1991.

Marconi, Joe. 1992. *Crisis Marketing: When Bad Things Happen to Good Companies*. Chicago: Probus Publishing.

Marconi, Joe. 1991. *Getting the Best from Your Ad Agency.* Chicago: Probus Publishing.

Mitroff, Ian and Thierry Panchant. 1990. *We're So Big and Powerful Nothing Bad Can Happen To Us.* New York: Birch Lane Press.

Ourusoff, Alexander, Paul B. Brown, and Jason Starr. "What's in a Name?" *Financial World,* September 1, 1992.

Poole, Claire. "Marketing Moocher." *Forbes,* September 16, 1991.

"Rethinking IDS from the Bottom Up." *Business Week,* February 8, 1993.

Ries, Al and Jack Trout. 1986. *Positioning: The Battle for Your Mind.* 2d ed. New York: McGraw Hill.

Ries, Al and Jack Trout. 1993. *The 22 Immutable Laws of Marketing.* New York: Harper Business.

Rutherford, Andrea C. "Candy Firms Roll Out 'Healthy' Sweets, but Snackers May Soon Sour on the Product." *The Wall Street Journal,* August 10, 1992.

Tedlow, Richard S. 1990. *New and Improved.* New York: Basic Books.

"The Most Powerful Brands in the World." In *Superbrands 1990.* New York: Adweek Magazine, 1990.

"They're Back!" *Advertising Age,* January 11, 1993.

"Time Management." *The Delaney Report,* February 16, 1992.

Torres, Craig. "Fading Brand-Name Loyalty Might Sway Investors." *The Wall Street Journal,* April 6, 1993.

Winters, Patricia. "Pepsi Max Sweetens Diet Cola Stakes." *Advertising Age,* March 8, 1993.

INDEX